Global Perspectives on Organizational Conflict

Global Perspectives on Organizational Conflict

———————— • ————————

Edited by
M. Afzalur Rahim
and
Albert A. Blum

PRAEGER

Westport, Connecticut
London

Library of Congress Cataloging-in-Publication Data

Global perspectives on organizational conflict / edited by M. Afzalur
    Rahim and Albert A. Blum.
       p.   cm.
    Includes bibliographical references and index.
    ISBN 0–275–93828–X (alk. paper)
    1. Conflict management—Cross-cultural studies. 2. Intergroup
relations—Cross-cultural studies.   I. Rahim, M. Afzalur.
  II. Blum, Albert A.
  HD42.G58   1994
  658.4—dc20   93–11874

British Library Cataloguing in Publication Data is available.

Library of Congress Catalog Card Number: 93–11874
ISBN: 0–275–93828–X

First published in 1994

Praeger Publishers, 88 Post Road West, Westport, CT 06881
An imprint of Greenwood Publishing Group, Inc.

Printed in the United States of America

The paper used in this book complies with the
Permanent Paper Standard issued by the National
Information Standards Organization (Z39.48–1984).

10 9 8 7 6 5 4 3 2 1

CONTENTS

Tables and Figures   vii

1. Introduction   1
   M. Afzalur Rahim and Albert A. Blum

2. France   11
   Christopher Leeds

3. Japan   33
   Robert T. Moran, Jonathan Allen, Richard Wichmann,
   Tomoko Ando, and Machiko Sasano

4. The Netherlands   53
   Ben Emans, Peter Laskewitz, and Evert van de Vliert

5. Norway   67
   Jørn Kjell Rognes

6. South Africa   87
   Frank M. Horwitz

7. Spain   103
   Lourdes Munduate, Juan Ganaza, Manuel Alcaide, and José M. Peiró

8. Turkey   135
   M. Kamil Kozan

Index 153

About the Editors and Contributors 159

TABLES AND FIGURES

Tables

1.1	Hofstede's Cultural Dimensions Classified by Country	3
3.1	Negotiation Styles of Japanese and Americans	48
7.1	Managerial Reference Group Norms of Style of Handling Interpersonal Conflict (Spain)	118
8.1	Means and Standard Deviations for Conflict Management Styles (Turkey)	144
8.2	Discriminant Analysis Results (Turkey)	145

Figures

1.1	A Two-Dimensional Model of Styles of Handling Interpersonal Conflict	5
1.2	Integrative and Distributive Dimensions of Styles of Handling Interpersonal Conflict	8
3.1	Model of Japanese Conflict Management	44
7.1	Styles of Handling Interpersonal Conflict (Spain)	121

1

INTRODUCTION

M. Afzalur Rahim and Albert A. Blum

Businesspeople, public servants, and students around the world are becoming increasingly concerned about how to manage conflict—that is, when conflict does result, how best to use whatever conflict-management strategies are available. Countries around the world deal with these topics differently. And yet businesspeople and others from one country have to deal with businesspeople and others in other countries. Therefore, they have to understand how other countries differ in negotiating strategies, in managing conflict, and in using alternative techniques to deal with disputes effectively. This book consists of chapters dealing with how seven major countries in the world deal with the above-mentioned topics, written by experts in the field. And, as a result, the readers, made up of businesspeople, public officials, and students will be better able to deal with those in their country as well as with those in other countries with whom they have to negotiate, manage conflicts, or, if necessary, be able to make use of dispute resolution techniques. Chapters 2–8 deal with conflict management in France, Japan, The Netherlands, Norway, South Africa, Spain, and Turkey. Each chapter contains five distinct sections:

1. *Social, Cultural, and Economic Factors*. Here the chapter authors discuss how various social, cultural, and economic forces affect conflict management. Since we felt that culture is one of the major factors that influence conflict-management styles (Ting-Toomey et al., 1991), each chapter contains discussion on this influence. To maintain consistency throughout the book, every chapter author used Hofstede's (1980) constructs of culture. Therefore, details of his theory have been provided later in this chapter.

2. *Managerial Styles*. This section deals with how managerial styles affect conflict management. A number of managerial styles, such as benevolent

autocratic, consultative, paternalistic, rule-following, and participative, were discussed.

3. *Styles of Handling Interpersonal Conflict.* Each chapter contains a discussion of the five styles of handling interpersonal conflict, such as *integrating, obliging, dominating, avoiding,* and *compromising,* which are selected and used by professionals to manage conflict in their organizations. To maintain consistency throughout the book, each chapter used these five-category conflict management styles. Therefore, a detailed discussion of the theory and research on these styles have been provided later in this chapter.

4. *Alternative Dispute Management.* This section deals with how alternative dispute management procedures are available in each country for the management of organizational conflict. These include mediation, conciliation, arbitration, ombudsman, nonjudicial conflict resolution, and social pacts.

5. *Discussion.* The chapter authors discuss conclusions and implications for improving managerial effectiveness and for future research. The chapter authors talk about what is needed in conflict management for organizations in their countries.

SOCIAL, CULTURAL, AND ECONOMIC FACTORS

In describing the cultural background that has influenced each country's conflict-management styles, authors have made extensive use of the work of Hofstede (1980). He compared a host of countries along four dimensions: *power distance, uncertainty avoidance, individualism, and masculinity.*

Power Distance

Hofstede describes the power distance dimension as "a measure of the interpersonal power or influence between a boss and a subordinate as perceived by the least powerful of the two, the subordinate" (p. 99). Different cultures maintain consistently different power distances in hierarchies. In high power-distance cultures subordinates consider themselves to be different from their supervisors, and authority-based relationships are tolerated. In low power-distance cultures people are more likely to believe that power should be used only when it is based on acknowledged position (legitimate power) or on what an individual knows or can do (expert power).

Uncertainty Avoidance

The uncertainty avoidance dimension is based on the extent to which people in a culture strive to avoid unstructured, unpredictable, or unclear situations. This index measures the norm for (in)tolerance of ambiguity. Cultures high in uncertainty avoidance develop strict codes of behavior and prefer to contain aggression by avoiding conflict and competition

Table 1.1
Hofstede's Cultural Dimensions Classified by Country

	Power Distance	Uncertainty Avoidance	Individualism	Masculinity
1. France	68	86	71	43
2. Japan	54	92	46	95
3. Netherlands	38	53	80	14
4. Norway	31	50	69	8
5. South Africa	49	49	65	63
6. Spain	57	86	51	42
7. Turkey	66	85	37	45
8. USA	40	46	91	62
Mean	50.38	68.38	63.75	46.50

Note: Values or work goal scores were computed for a stratified sample of seven occupations at two points in time (Hofstede, 1980, pp. 104, 165, 222, 279).

within their group. Members of cultures low in uncertainty avoidance are more tolerant of ambiguity, seek change more, and are more likely to accept dissent and risk-taking.

Individualism

Broadly, this dimension describes the relationship between the individual and the collectivity that exists in a given society. In individualistic cultures the goals of the individual are emphasized over the goals of the group. Self-realization is given precedence over group well-being, and self-advancement is encouraged over group harmony. People in individualistic cultures are supposed to take care of themselves and their immediate families, whereas in collectivistic cultures people belong to in-groups (such as extended family, coworkers, and social and religious organizations) that take care of them in exchange for the individual's loyalty to the group's goals, needs, and views. In collectivistic cultures, mutual interdependence is fostered rather than independence. In addition, members of collectivist cultures tend to draw sharper delineations between in-group and out-group members.

Masculinity

The masculinity dimension is based on the extent to which there is sex-role differentiation in the culture. Those cultures high on the masculinity scale emphasize highly differentiated sex roles, view work as more central to their lives, and emphasize material success and assertiveness. In cultures low on the masculinity dimension, "feminine" values such as quality of life, interpersonal relationships, and fluid sex roles predominate.

In the discussions in Chapters 2–8, it has been shown that the seven countries score differently on the four dimensions of culture, and, as a result, in general react differently to conflict situations. For example, people in a country that scores high on uncertainty avoidance will more likely avoid conflict, while people in a country low in uncertainty avoidance would be more likely to accept the risk of conflict. Where each of the countries (including the United States) stands on Hofstede scales is shown in Table 1.1.

STYLES OF HANDLING INTERPERSONAL CONFLICT

Since each chapter has used the conceptualizations of the five styles of handling interpersonal conflict, as stated above, we felt that there should be a detailed discussion of them. This part uses a micro approach in the sense that discussions in each chapter indicate how individual managers handle their interpersonal conflict in their organizations. The chapters on Italy and Turkey provide some data on conflict management styles.

The five styles of handling interpersonal conflict have become very popular in teaching and research. This is evident from the number of recent doctoral dissertations (e.g., Keenan, 1984; Levy, 1989; Neff, 1986; Persico, 1986; van Epps, 1990) and other empirical studies (e.g., Lee, 1990; Pilkington, Richardson, & Utley, 1988; Psenicka & Rahim, 1989; Rahim & Buntzman, 1988; Ting-Toomey et al., 1991; van de Vliert & Kabanoff, 1990) that have utilized the conceptualization and operationalization of the five styles.

The five styles of handling interpersonal conflict in organizations was first suggested by Mary P. Follett (1926/1940). She found three principal ways of dealing with conflict, such as domination, compromise, and integration; and two other ways of handling conflict in organizations, such as avoidance and suppression. Blake and Mouton (1964) first presented a conceptualization for classifying the modes (styles) for handling interpersonal conflicts into five types: forcing, withdrawing, smoothing, compromising, and problem solving. They described the five modes of handling conflict on the basis of the attitudes of the manager: concern for production and for people. This was reinterpreted by Thomas (1992), who considered the intentions of a party (cooperativeness—attempting to satisfy the other party's concerns; and assertiveness—attempting to satisfy one's own concerns) in classifying the modes of handling conflict into five types.

Using a conceptualization similar to the above theorists, the styles of handling conflict were differentiated on two basic dimensions: concern for self and for others (Rahim, 1983a, c; Rahim, 1992; Rahim & Bonoma, 1979). The first dimension explains the degree (high or low) to which a person attempts to satisfy his or her own concern. The second dimension explains the degree (high or low) to which an organizational member attempts to satisfy the concern of others. It should be pointed out that these dimensions portray the motivational orientations of a given individual during conflict. A study by van de Vliert and Kabanoff (1990; see also Ruble & Thomas, 1976) provided support for these dimensions. Combination of the two dimensions results in five specific styles of handling interpersonal conflict, as shown in Figure 1.1.

Integrating: High Concern for Self and Others

This style involves collaboration between the parties for problem solving. This requires trust and openness so that the parties can exchange in-

Figure 1.1
A Two-Dimensional Model of Styles of Handling Interpersonal Conflict

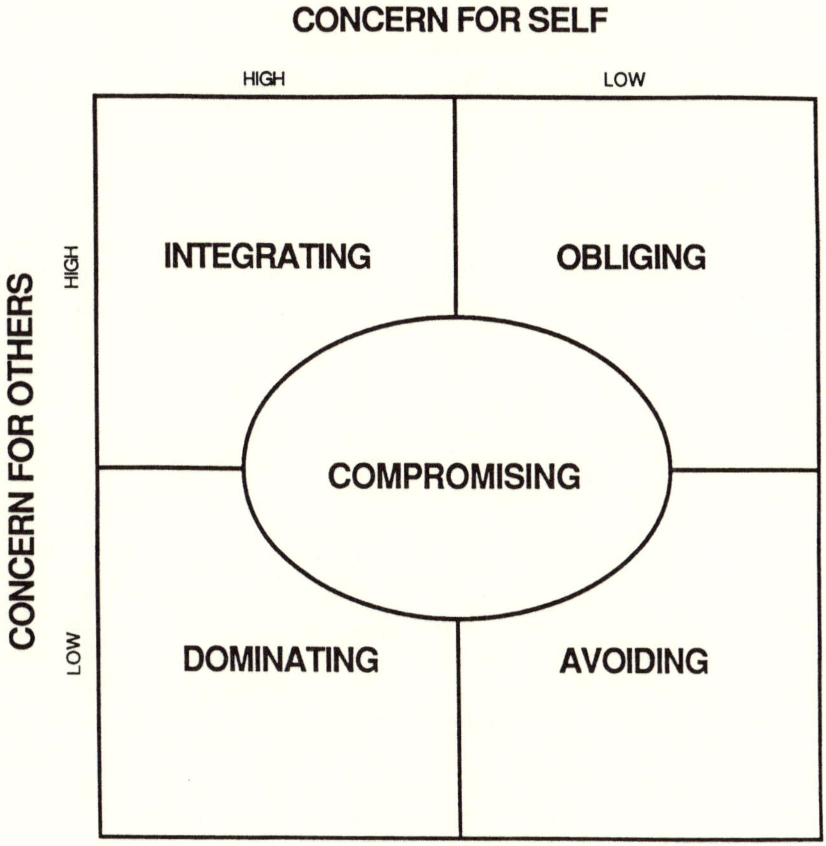

formation and analyze their differences to reach a solution acceptable to them. "The first rule . . . for obtaining integration is to put your cards on the table, face the real issue, uncover the conflict, bring the whole thing into the open" (Follett, 1940, p. 38). Implementation of "Follett's rule" is possible if the parties trust each other. Prein (1976) suggested that this style has two distinctive elements: confrontation and problem solving. Confrontation involves open and direct communication, which should make way for problem solving. As a result, it may lead to creative solutions to problems.

Obliging: Low Concern for Self and High Concern for Others

This style is associated with attempting to play down the differences and emphasizing similarities to satisfy the concern of the other party. It may take the form of self-sacrifice, selfless generosity, charity, or obedience to another person's wishes. An obliging person neglects his or her own concern to satisfy the concern of the other party. Such an individual is like a "conflict absorber," that is, a "person whose reaction to a perceived hostile act on the part of another has low hostility or even positive friendliness" (Boulding, 1962, p. 171).

Dominating: High Concern for Self and Low Concern for Others

This style has been identified with win-lose orientation or with competing behavior to win one's position. A dominating or competing person goes all out to win his or her objective and, as a result, often ignores the needs and expectations of the other party. Dominating may mean standing up for one's rights and/or defending a position that the party believes to be correct. Sometimes a dominating person wants to win at any cost. A dominating supervisor is likely to use his or her position power to impose his or her will on subordinates and command their obedience.

Avoiding: Low Concern for Self and Others

This style has been associated with ignoring, withdrawal, sidestepping, or "see no evil, hear no evil, speak no evil" situations. It may take the form of postponing an issue until a better time, or simply withdrawing from a threatening situation. An avoiding person fails to satisfy his or her own needs as well as the needs of the other party. This style is often characterized by an unconcerned attitude toward the issues or parties involved in conflict. Such a person may refuse to acknowledge in public that there is a conflict that should be dealt with.

Compromising: Intermediate in Concern for Self and Others

This style involves give-and-take or sharing, whereby both parties give up something to make a mutually acceptable decision. It may mean splitting the difference, exchanging concession, or seeking a quick middle-ground position. A compromising party gives up more than a dominating party but less than an obliging party. Likewise, such a party addresses an issue more directly than an avoiding party, but does not explore it in as much depth as an integrating party.

Additional insights may be gained by reclassifying the five styles of handling interpersonal conflict according to the terminologies of the game theory. Integrating style can be reclassified to positive-sum or nonzero-sum (win-win) style, compromising to mixed (no-win/no-lose) style, and obliging, dominating, and avoiding to zero-sum or negative-sum (lose-win, win-lose, and lose-lose, respectively) style. In general, positive-sum and, to some extent mixed, styles are appropriate for dealing with the strategic issues. The zero-sum styles can be used to deal with tactical, day-to-day, or routine problems (Rahim, 1985).

Further insights into the five styles of handling interpersonal conflict may be obtained by organizing them according to the integrative and distributive dimensions of labor-management bargaining suggested by Walton and McKersie (1965). The two dimensions are represented by the heavy lines in the diagonals of Figure 1.2.

The integrative dimension (integrating-avoiding) represents the degree (high or low) of satisfaction of concerns received by self and others. The distributive dimension (dominating-obliging) represents the proportion of the satisfaction of concerns received by self and others (Rahim, 1992). In the integrative dimension, integrating attempts to increase the satisfaction of the concerns of both parties by finding unique solutions to the problems acceptable to them. Avoiding leads to the reduction of satisfaction of the concerns of both parties as a result of their failure to confront and solve their problems. In the distributive dimension, whereas dominating attempts to obtain high satisfaction of concerns for self (and provide low satisfaction of concerns for others), obliging attempts to obtain low satisfaction of concerns for self (and provide high satisfaction of concerns for others). Compromising represents the point of intersection of the two dimensions—that is, a middle-ground position where each party receives an intermediate level of satisfaction of their concerns from the resolution of their conflicts. Thomas (1992) recognized that the above design for conceptualizing the styles of handling interpersonal conflict is a noteworthy improvement over the simple cooperative-competitive dichotomy suggested by Deutsch (1949, 1990). This design is also an improvement over the three and four styles of handling conflict proposed by Putnam and Wilson (1982) and Pruitt (1983), respectively (van de Vliert & Kabanoff, 1990; Rahim, 1991).

Figure 1.2
**Integrative and Distributive Dimensions of Styles of Handling
Interpersonal Conflict**

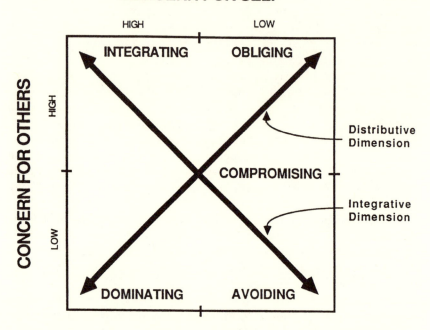

CONCERN FOR SELF

Ting-Toomey et al.'s (1991) cross-cultural study provided evidence that the five styles of handling interpersonal conflict, as measured by the Rahim Organizational Conflict Inventory–II (Rahim, 1983b), significantly differed among five cultures (countries): United States, Japan, China, South Korea, and Taiwan. Ting-Toomey et al. (1991) reported that "culture influences conflict styles—with the U.S. respondents reporting the use of a higher degree of dominating conflict style than the Japanese and Korean respondents, and the Chinese and Taiwanese respondents reporting the use of a higher degree of obliging and avoiding styles than the U.S. respondents" (p. 289). This study also reported that culture explained 54 percent of the variance in the set of five conflict management styles (p. 290).

It appears that culture may determine how the two dimensions of conflict-management styles—distributive and integrative—are selected and used. Whereas organizational members from individualistic cultures may select distributive dimension to resolve their interpersonal conflict, organizational members from collectivistic cultures may select and use integrative dimension for managing this conflict. Future research should try to investigate how organizational members from different cultures select and use the two dimensions of conflict styles. Future studies should also investigate the effectiveness of the five styles in different cultures.

REFERENCES

Blake, R. R., & Mouton, J. S. (1964). *The managerial grid*. Houston: Gulf.

Boulding, K. E. (1962). *Conflict and defense: A general theory*. New York: Harper & Row.

Deutsch, M. (1949). A theory of cooperation and competition. *Human Relations, 2,* 129–151.

Deutsch, M. (1990). Sixty years of conflict. *International Journal of Conflict Management, 1,* 237–263.

Follett, M. P. (1926/1940). Constructive conflict. In H. C. Metcalf & L. Urwick (Eds.), *Dynamic administration: The collected papers of Mary Parker Follet* (pp. 30–49). New York: Harper & Row [original work published in 1926].

Hofstede, G. (1980). *Culture's consequences: International differences in work-related values*. Beverly Hills, CA: Sage.

Keenan, D. (1984). *A study to determine the relationship between organizational climates and management styles of conflict as perceived by teachers and principals in selected school districts*. Unpublished doctoral dissertation, West Virginia University.

Lee, C.-W. (1990). Relative role and styles of handling interpersonal conflict: An experimental study with Korean managers. *International Journal of Conflict Management, 1,* 327–340.

Levy, M. B. (1989). *Integration of lovestyles and attachment styles: Cross-partner influences and a clarification of concepts, measurement, and conceptualization*. Unpublished doctoral dissertation, University of South Carolina.

Neff, E. K. (1986). *Conflict management styles of women administrators in the 12 state universities in Ohio*. Unpublished doctoral dissertation, Bowling Green State University, Ohio.

Persico, J., Jr. (1986). *Levels of conflict, worker performance, individual conflict styles, type of work organizational characteristics and the external environment of the organization*. Unpublished doctoral dissertation, University of Minnesota.

Pilkington, C. J., Richardson, D. R., & Utley, M. E. (1988). Is conflict stimulating? Sensation seekers' responses to interpersonal conflict. *Personality and Social Psychology Bulletin, 14,* 596–603.

Prein, H.C.M. (1976). Stijlen van conflicthantering [Styles of handling conflict]. *Nederlands Tijdschrift voor de Psychologie, 31,* 321–346.

Pruitt, D. G. (1983). Strategic choice in negotiation. *American Behavioral Scientist, 27,* 167–194.

Psenicka, C., & Rahim, M. A. (1989). Integrative and distributive dimensions of styles of handling interpersonal conflict and bargaining outcome. In M. A. Rahim (Ed.), *Managing conflict: An interdisciplinary approach* (pp. 33–40). New York: Praeger.

Putnam, L. L., & Wilson, C. E. (1982). Communicative strategies in organizational conflicts: Reliability and validity of a measurement scale. In M. Burgoon (Ed.), *Communication yearbook 6* (pp. 629–652). Beverly Hills, CA: Sage.

Rahim, M. A. (1983a). A measure of styles of handling interpersonal conflict. *Academy of Management Journal, 26*, 368–376.

Rahim, M. A. (1983b). *Rahim Organizational Conflict Inventory–II*. Palo Alto, CA: Consulting Psychologists Press.

Rahim, M. A. (1983c). *Rahim Organizational Conflict Inventories: Professional manual*. Palo Alto, CA: Consulting Psychologists Press.

Rahim, M. A. (1985). A strategy for managing conflict in complex organizations. *Human Relations, 38*, 81–89.

Rahim, M. A. (1991, June). *Styles of handling interpersonal conflict: A critical review of theory and research*. Paper presented at the 4th annual conference of the International Association for Conflict Management, Dan Dolder, Netherlands.

Rahim, M. A. (1992). *Managing conflict in organizations* (2nd ed.). Westport, CT: Praeger.

Rahim, A., & Bonoma, T. V. (1979). Managing organizational conflict: A model for diagnosis and intervention. *Psychological Reports, 44*, 1323–1344.

Rahim, M. A., & Buntzman, G. F. (1988). Supervisory power bases, styles of handling conflict with subordinates, and subordinate compliance and satisfaction. *Journal of Psychology, 123*, 195–210.

Ruble, T. L., & Thomas, K. W. (1976). Support for a two-dimensional model of conflict behavior. *Organizational Behavior and Human Performance, 16*, 143–155.

Thomas, K. W. (1992). Conflict and negotiation processes in organizations. In M. D. Dunnette & L. M. Hough (Eds.), *Handbook of industrial & organizational psychology*, Vol. 3 (2nd ed., pp. 651–717). Palo Alto, CA: Consulting Psychologists Press.

Ting-Toomey, S., Gao, G., Trubisky, P., Yang, Z., Kim, H. S., Lin, S.-L., & Nishida, T. (1991). Culture, face maintenance, and styles of handling interpersonal conflict: A study in five cultures. *International Journal of Conflict Management, 2*, 275–296.

van de Vliert, E., & Kabanoff, B. (1990). Toward theory based measures of conflict management. *Academy of Management Journal, 33*, 199–209.

van Epps, P. D. (1990). *Conflict management style preferences predicted by psychological androgyny and managerial frames of reference*. Unpublished doctoral dissertation, University of New Orleans, LA.

Walton, R. E., & McKersie, R. B. (1965). *A behavioral theory of labor negotiations: An analysis of social interaction system*. New York: McGraw-Hill.

2

FRANCE

Christopher Leeds

This chapter focuses on medium and large industrial companies and their main characteristics that affect negotiations and conflict management. In many ways these industrial organizations have similar features to other large entities in France, such as branches of the Civil Service and the public sector, including higher education. The explanation lies partly in the persuasiveness and strength of French culture, traditions, and habits (Exiga et al., 1981, pp. 18–19). Another factor is the continued preponderance of former civil servants (many being ex-graduates of top prestigious Grandes Ecoles such as Le Polytechnique) in the management of important French companies. Naturally, significant differences also separate businesses from other organizations.

The French have been adept in blending within their culture contrasting traits of neighboring North European and Mediterranean cultures. Large industrial companies maintain a delicate balance between systematic and organic structures and procedures. To a considerable degree systematic reflects the formal system, and traits associated with low context and individualist, while organic reflects the informal, and traits associated with high context and collectivist.

Since 1936 the failure of companies to resolve serious industrial conflicts resulted in regular state intervention. State pressure or legislation led to businesses instituting more effective methods for handling conflicts, particularly after 1968. Alternative dispute procedures have grown in importance since the 1960s. The most successful forms have been "informal" public-sector mediation and the seeking of help from private agencies, rather than from official conciliatory procedures.

Today autocratic, particularly paternalist, management styles are less important. Greater emphasis is placed on forms of consultative management, especially at lower management and supervisory levels, and on allowing employees greater autonomy and freedom to express their views openly. In addition the informal systems and organic structures have increasingly been recognized by management as the most effective way through which to handle conflicts, particularly if in latent form (conflict prevention).

Dominating and avoiding negotiating styles used to be the dominant forms practiced by superiors when dealing with subordinates in interpersonal conflicts. Since 1968 the integrating style, and the French variant of dialogue (*la concertation*) has been employed to a greater degree, and also various styles known only to the French, devised to suit particular circumstances.

ECONOMIC, SOCIAL, AND CULTURAL FACTORS

France is one of the two largest countries, together with Germany, in the European Community, with a population of about 57.2 million. Although the population density is 101 per square kilometer, much of the land is sparsely inhabited, since a third of the population lives in the Paris area and the bulk of the rest in the sixteen largest regional centers such as Marseilles, Lyons, and Lille. France has the fourth largest economy of the countries in the Organization for Economic Cooperation and Development.

In recent years cross-cultural and conflict theorists have shown that many ideas on management, organizations, and the styles of handling conflict are primarily culture-specific rather than being universally applicable, since considerable variation and divergences exist across countries and cultures (Lee & Rogan, 1991, p. 182; Gruère & Morel, 1991, p. 21; Hofstede, 1991, p. 238).

Among the French, considerable variation in character and temperament exists. This is partly because France is a land of contrasts and diversity, as reflected in its geography, history, and culture. One major division is between the north, originally occupied by Germanic tribes, and the south, inhabited from an early period by Mediterranean people. Another is the distinction between the western area, which shares an Atlantic tradition with Northern Europe, and Eastern France, influenced culturally by neighboring countries.

One noticeable result of this variation is the contradictory strain in the mentality and behavior of the different groups. This ambivalence is reflected in the relations between the individual and the state, and between industrial employers and employees. As a result, French society as a whole and also specific organizations tend to maintain an equilibrium between contrasting tendencies, which are explained later. Examples are the counterforces of centralization-individualism, control-autonomy, systematic-organic, and formal-informal practices.

Usually systematic (mechanistic) and organic organizations are considered contrasting types. These terms are not necessarily interchangeable with the labels "formal-informal." However, France, placed at a midpoint along the systematic-organic dimension with reference to European countries (Mole, 1990, pp. 180, 182), possesses industrial organizations both highly systematic formally, combined with various degrees of informal organic practices. Mole's positioning of France is confirmed by the findings of various French researchers who place France in some mid-position on *related* dimensions concerning low-high context and monochronic-polychronic cultures (Gruère & Morel, 1990, p. 16).

Systematic organizations tend to be monochronic (people generally doing one thing at a time) and task-oriented. Staff are low-context, needing substantial information before carrying out tasks, being little accustomed to operating by unwritten rules and codes. In contrast, people in organic structures are likely to be polychronic, prepared to do several things at once, and to being interrupted. They are high-context. Their close involvement in various informal networks keeps them up-to-date on essentials, so they are less reliant on official information sources (Hall & Hall, 1990, p. 14).

Hofstede places the Hall low- and high-context categories as one of a pair of subfeatures of his individualism-collectivism dimension. In principle he is right to do this. In the case of France, however, the problem is that while the works of both Hofstede and Mole show France as highly individualistic, it is not primarily low-context but moderately low- and high-context.

Low and high power distance and masculinity-femininity are two more Hofstede dimensions. French individualism combined with medium power distance in business partly explain why the French tend to prefer individual rather than group decision-making. However, France's attachment to family traditions and consensus-building also reflects the collectivist tradition, stronger in the south than the north, and France's ranking as a moderate feminine culture. In business these aspects can be seen in the custom of holding meetings that function in a quasi-consultative role and for achieving group harmony and agreement prior to, or after, important company or departmental decisions have been taken. The collectivist influence is one of the factors explaining why the French are partly high context.

Although individualism-collectivism is only one of Hofstede's cultural dimensions, other researchers have considered this particular dimension as the most significant for analyzing cultural differences in conflict behavior internationally (Ting-Toomey et al., 1991, p. 276; Lee & Rogan, 1991, p. 185). However, in relation to France, this author feels that the systematic-organic dimension is particularly helpful for identifying some of the contrasting characteristics of French business culture and the handling of conflict.

Past Roman unifying traditions, their codified law, and long hierarchical structures influenced the way French government policies of centraliza- tion were implemented from the seventeenth century. The state has always been ready to provide strong direction, acting as a unifying agency against counterforces fostering particularism, individualism, or secession. The French experts in creating systematic systems included Colbert, Louis XIV's finance minister, and Napoleon Bonaparte. The particular adminis- trative practices, as built up by governments and the Civil Service, influ- ence French behavior in all organizations, including businesses (Gruère & Morel, 1991, p. 57).

Systematic cultures emphasize prescribed structures and a *fait accompli* approach to certain values and traditions, which people are socialized into accepting. Cultural values that have a profound influence in France in- clude elements relating first to order, such as the importance of laws and rules, procedures, functions; second to the intellect or education, including the importance given to science, mathematics, to acquiring a logical ap- proach to life, and qualifications (Vachette, 1984, p. 121). Certain modern German attitudes and practices stemming from the systematic mode, rather than the organic practices of earlier immigrant Germanic tribes that came to France when the Romans departed, have also influenced how French cultural values have evolved.

Cross-cultural researchers such as Hofstede (1991, p. 113) have stressed certain cultural elements of the French such as (1) the acceptance of medium power distance or disparities, as reflected in the moderately steep pyramidal nature of their organizations; (2) the acceptance of a depen- dency relationship; and (3) the desire for predictability and the avoidance of uncertainty. These, combined with certain other traits such as the iden- tification with the cult of the hero or charismatic leadership (Vachette, 1984, p. 120), help to explain the French attachment to a well-ordered, sys- tematic organization.

The law reinforces the extensive powers of the chief executive of a com- pany. Recent works stress that the ideal leader is still regarded as someone akin to the "enlightened despot" or "good father" (Hofstede, 1991, pp. 25–26; Gruère & Morel, 1990, p. 36; Barsoux & Lawrence, 1990, p. 78). Man- agers like to centralize decision-making and are reluctant to delegate. De- cisions of a certain nature are usually taken at a higher level than in Anglo-Saxon countries. Consequently most medium and large French in- dustrial organizations are still structured in a traditional, classical, or Tay- lorian mode combined with autocratic or paternalist leadership.

On Hofstede's fourth dimension, weak to strong uncertainty avoidance, France is ranked toward the latter end of the dimension. The French desire for certainty, for avoiding conflict, or even for preventing problems or con- flict occurring is reflected in their attachment to rules, their formalism, and their approach to communications. The typical businessperson appreciates having clear descriptions of the company he or she works for, including a detailed organization chart. All arrangements, even of a minor nature, are invariably formalized in writing, and internal communications tend to take written forms so as to minimize embarrassing encounters. Concrete proof exists that avoids unnecessary arguments later. Importance is attached to etiquette and protocol. First-naming is rare at work and humor sparsely employed for easing tension. A humorous person is regarded as flippant, and so humor is largely confined to private life. The French tend to be professional and perfectionist in matters pertaining to style, dress, manners, and forms of address.

The state plays an important role in industry, since many company regulations and procedures stem directly from laws. Even the origin of the French term for manager (*cadre*) dates from a 1936 law. The state, anxious to soften the confrontational boss-worker relationship in the business world, required firms to create an intermediary managerial level. In that year all organizations (public or private) of fifty or more employees were required by law to create a works' committee (*comité d'établissement*) composed of representatives (*délégues du personnel*) of different sections at work. These committees meet monthly and perform a consultative role in dealing with complaints about work conditions.

Despite the continued existence of traditional management in many companies today, employees cannot be treated arbitrarily. They are protected by a comprehensive system of laws concerning work conditions, job security, welfare, rights, and so on as contained in their *statut* (the rough equivalent of the American contract). If a person fails to work properly after repeated warnings, he or she is unlikely to be fired (an expensive procedure) but moved to another department (d' Iribarne, 1989, p. 24). The French are preoccupied with status and rank. Qualifications, rather than experience or personal ability, are vital in determining the level at which new applicants enter a firm, and for major promotions.

The importance given to rank, status, titles, and hierarchy in French companies often leads to certain tensions within the superior-subordinate relationship. The latter tends to be one of giving and obeying orders rather than of relaxed cooperation between partners. A subordinate respects a superior but fears making mistakes, while the superior fears criticism. The French have been accustomed, often in business or elsewhere, to arbitrary or personal leadership that creates dependency behavior and an unwillingness to take risks by subordinates.

The preference for order, stability, and dependency means that the French allow considerable power to governments. However, the authorities are sometimes slow and inflexible in handling problems, which results in conflicts remaining unsolved and latent. Further, the government habitually imposes major plans or projects on people or organizations without first consulting those involved.

Restrictions, burdens, policies, and rules imposed on the French by the state or employers provide the dynamism, it has been argued, for the development of many elements of French individualism (an important aspect of French organic practices). These include the love of challenge, the rejection of restrictions, a defiant attitude toward authority, and the practice known as System D (*débrouillardise* or self-reliance). The latter signifies the Frenchman's ability to cope, if leadership flounders, or when not closely supervised. System D also reflects the tendency to adapt or ignore laws, orders, or procedures, literally or explicitly, if they seem irrelevant or impractical (Comp-Langlois, 1984, p. 123; Vachette, 1984, p. 120).

The French, like other Latin peoples, are inclined to be ambivalent in attitude toward authority or employers (Vachette, 1984, p. 120). They look to the state for help in need, and yet distrust politicians who impose constraints. When a point is reached when government policies are no longer bearable, the French tend to change from an attitude of acquiescence to one of total resistance, joining together spontaneously, as reflected in past political upheavals or industrial unrest—modern examples being 1936 and 1968. Initial polarized confrontational positions then give way to flexible strategies by governments willing to resolve most of the outstanding popular grievances.

Many industrial companies are frequently less rigid in their work procedures than appears to be the case on the surface, especially since the late 1960s. French capacity in creating systematic structures is matched by their ability in evading or supplementing them with parallel informal practices (d'Iribarne, 1989, p. 258). An element of this dual systematic-organic tradition is symbolized in the practice traceable to pre-1789 French administrations of a "strict rule but a lenient practice" (*une règle rigide, une pratique molle*) (Hofstede, 1991, p. 121).

In countries where people commonly create rules and procedures that fit particular groups and circumstances, the organic approach, as in Greece and Latin countries (Mole, 1990, p. 188), informal or unofficial practices are likely to be more important than formal procedures. Elements in the French culture and character, such as the respect for individualism and acceptance of nonconformism, draws them toward ad hoc or pragmatic procedures. French organizations have been called opaque, a description that reflects the importance of hidden implicit rules and tacit understandings. French businesses tend to have a certain natural slack, flexibility, and looseness (called *flue*) and grey areas where responsibilities are blurred (Barsoux & Lawrence, 1990, p. 156). Certain jobs may lack detailed descriptions, while unofficial job titles may exist.

Many French tend to be intuitive, high context, as described earlier, and adept at befriending others who privately communicate vital information. This is necessary because normal hierarchical channels, reporting structures, or formal procedures of coordination are frequently neither very developed nor much respected. Managers may only share specialized or vital information with colleagues who belong to their private network (Hall & Hall, 1991, p. 115). Superiors may deny information to subordinates but expect them to be informed about what to do. Vertical communications tend to take indirect forms associated with social codes and traditions as well as rules. As subordinates may not report regularly to superiors, groups often cooperate horizontally in settling problems (d'Iribarne, 1989, p. 54; Gruère & Morel, 1991, p. 31).

A complicated network of informal alliances binds groups of workers doing similar tasks. These tacit ententes operate as a microculture, establishing their own rules, practices, and values, and defending their group interests (Sainsaulieu, 1987, p. 150). There is little sense in France of team spirit, understood in Britain as a positive force covering a whole unit. Instead the group tends to be seen as a negative or clannish force (*l'ésprit de clan*).

Obviously the degree of autonomy allowed to subordinates may vary depending on management style and other factors. In general the French resent being closely monitored. Consequently supervisors usually allow discretion in how orders are carried out and performance appraisal techniques are rarely used. Considerable autonomy is usually given by head offices to branches. Autonomy, it is claimed, allows French organizations to function with a minimum of effort or coordination (d'Iribarne, 1989, p. 97). In an American company the general feeling is that everybody works for someone else, whereas in a French company employees like to imagine they work for themselves, answerable only to their conscience or "sense of honor" (d'Iribarne, 1989, p. 22)

Power is a vital notion for the French, as for other Latin peoples. The organization slack in French companies facilitates power struggles, especially as employees like to maintain some uncertainty around their function. Managers who lose power conflicts tend to be isolated, humiliated, and deprived of information (*mettre au placard* or "put in the cupboard"). In one survey Latin managers agreed to a higher extent than Anglo-Saxon managers with the statement: "Most managements seem to be more motivated by gaining power than by achieving objectives—Agreed: U.S.A. 13%, Britain 30%, France 59%, Italy 59% (Laurent, 1986, p. 94).

Rather than being bound by a set of rules, and functional notions of authority, many French managers prefer to adopt a personalist or social approach to their organizations. Authority and power are regarded as stemming directly from the person exercising them, rather than from his or her role or as coming from someone higher up the organization (Laurent, 1986, pp. 95–96; Hofstede, 1991, p. 151). This implies that how tasks are executed depends particularly on personal interactions. One consequence is that when conflicts arise the people involved tend to indulge in personal recriminations, blaming each other rather than the system for errors made.

In the event of strong disagreement, a subordinate may refuse to obey his or her superior. Opposition is not seen invariably as indiscipline, but rather as a warning that the system itself may not be legitimate. One comparative study found that, out of ten European countries, French employees came next to last, only 25 percent of them replying "Yes" to the question asking whether they automatically carried out instructions. In answer to the second question: "I will only follow the instructions of my superior when my reason is convinced," the French were first with 57 percent replying "Yes." These replies reflect the independent-mindedness of the French and the need to communicate instructions in ways most likely to elicit the cooperation of subordinates (Barsoux & Lawrence, 1990, p. 7).

Organic elements reflect the fact that the French are aware of power dimensions and the personal or "people" aspect of life and work. In addition the ad hoc individualist tradition implies that the negotiator frequently prefers to evolve his or her own style, which may or may not fit any particular known category.

Predictably, in view of what has just been said, the French have also been ambivalent in their approach to negotiating. Even the process of negotiating used to be seen largely negatively, as merely a power struggle in which the outcomes were a confrontational stalemate, dominating (win-lose), a compromised position where objectives were abandoned in the bargaining process, or terminating the negotiating process.

An explanation is obviously imperative for this attitude. Some French regard negotiating as counter to logic and the Cartesian mind, a form of thinking based on the ideas of René Descartes, to which a large number of French students are exposed in their pre-Baccalauréat studies. For many French people the truth is unequivocal, to be discovered by reasoning. If one side is right, then the other side must be wrong (Gruère & Morel, 1991, p. 59). At various international conferences in the past, the rigidity of French participants has been observed: their practice of carefully preparing their positions in advance, which they believe logically will suit all parties; their dislike of bargaining; and their tendency to avoid or abandon negotiations if their standpoint is not accepted. In business, attitudes such as these were reflected in the autocratic manner in which staff were treated and management-employee relations conducted.

However, the contradictions in French behavior are shown in their changed positions at the informal level. The French are often flexible both regarding aims and the negotiating techniques applied. They are often unpredictable, and sensitive to particular situations and circumstances and to how people relate to each other (Hall & Hall, 1991, pp. 121, 133). In business, as in diplomacy, these attitudes are shown at the private unofficial discussions between small groups (in contrast to the public official meetings) that try to break deadlocks and find acceptable face-saving formulas and win-win solutions.

MANAGERIAL STYLES

Leadership styles vary markedly, especially when a business is only in one location, and this can be unsettling and counterproductive (Linhart, 1990, pp. 91–92). If a company has a strong all-pervasive culture, then one style is more likely to predominate. Sizable French companies today tend to be heterogeneous in their internal culture, granting considerable autonomy to various levels or branches, which may be scattered, at some distance from the parent organization. A distinction is often made between traditional or individual management styles, and collective or modern styles—namely, participative and communicative management.

Before 1939, and to a lesser extent until the late 1960s, the style of management was autocratic or paternalist. Various laws from 1950 had little success in encouraging workers, employers, and unions to negotiate collective agreements. The strongest union, the Communist-led Confédération Générale du Travail, viewed negotiation as capitulation and industrial relations as a class struggle. Irreconcilable, ideological differences were highlighted by management and workers or unions as factors that prevented them from meeting, or from resolving problems when they did.

Employers generally refused to negotiate with their staff, and employer-worker relations remained mostly one of separation (Touzard, 1977, p. 94). Management supplemented the policy of avoiding dialogue by imposing its ideas autocratically on the work force. The rigid social stratification at work between managers and workers institutionalized mutual distrust (Linhart, 1990, pp. 83–84).

Workers had no constructive outlets for their conflicts, which tended to rest latent until a crisis occurred, when management and workers became locked into a confrontational situation. Workers either adopted a withdrawal strategy or, alternatively, whether unionized or not, followed the unions when the latter went on strike. Strikes were usually brief but workers often resorted to extralegal measures, such as the occupation of premises and destruction of personnel records, to obtain their demands by force.

Since the major 1968 political disturbances in Paris, the strongly autocratic industrial employers have largely disappeared. However, most French companies still retain the traditional business structure and at least in formal relations a quasi-autocratic leadership style. However, industrial leaders were now more realistic and wished to prevent future mass industrial unrest by dealing with conflicts in their early stages. Assertive hands-on, competent, forward-looking chief executives soon became highly prized who could dynamize their work force and prevent dysfunctional conflicts erupting. The aim was also to break old confrontational and no-dialogue habits and to encourage direct superior-subordinate discussions, instead of workers looking to unions or others for handling conflicts.

Organic elements became more evident from the early 1970s, as industrial managers showed more flexibility and sensitivity to other people's viewpoints, being influenced by new ideas on management from abroad. Subordinates now had greater leeway in implementing their own ways of carrying out tasks.

A common view is that paternalism declines in importance inversely with the size of the firm, being largely confined to smaller firms. However, this is not entirely the case in France. The fostering of the family spirit has been considered as "one of the strengths of French management" (Comp-Langlois, 1984, p. 123; Sainsaulieu, 1987, p. 159). The positive aspects of paternalism include many elements of a feminine culture, such as focus on people problems rather than primarily on tasks, as reflected in the emphasis on employment security, and fostering superior-subordinate relationships (Hofstede, 1991, p. 82).

An important number of large companies, often efficient and innovative, such as L'Oreal, De Wendel, Schneider, Peugeot, Michelin, and Pont-A-Mousson, are still, in part, paternalist. The employer tries to protect the staff. To maintain its goal of life-long employment, Michelin used to adopt measures such as the creation of *voie de garages* or "sidings for burnt-out managers" (Barsoux & Lawrence, 1990, p. 156). Many department heads in French companies were still paternalist in the early 1980s, according to one study, thriving on being relied upon, creating dependency relations, and being able to supply answers to questions from subordinates (Laurent, 1986, p. 94). However, really negative aspects of paternalism, associated with conservative management, and leaders wishing to create conformists of their subordinates (Blake & Mouton, 1985, p. 141) are practices that became largely extinct after 1936.

Two leadership styles that are found most frequently at middle or lower management levels are the institutional or management style (*la style gestionnaire*) and the technocratic (*la technocratie*). The former is clearly recognizable in certain companies (Lebei, 1985, p. 123) where efforts are made to balance both task and people needs. The institutional manager makes effective use of informal information networks and develops personal relationships. The technocratic management style is based on Saint-Simon's ideas in the early nineteenth century. As firms became more cost-conscious and capital-intensive in the 1970s, so this form grew in significance, associated notably with the research and development sections of larger firms, or companies involved in high technology and scientific research. Individuals are generally highly qualified; they work independently on specialized projects or supervise complex machinery, maintain professional standards, and collaborate with few colleagues. Tension can arise because little social interaction occurs (d'Iribarne, 1989, p. 264; Exiga et al., 1981, p. 60).

Some French writers have shown management styles and organizations as progressing from traditional or individual forms toward modern forms including the participative (Fauvet, 1974, p. 41). In essence participative management assumes no inherent contradiction between company aims and the needs of staff or individual goals (Blake & Mouton, 1985, p. 82). Numerous French books and other publications advocate this form, or cite case studies of companies that have reduced their hierarchies, and improved internal communications.

Today very few French businesses of any size are fully participative. Certainly an important number of medium to large companies, influenced by developments in the United States and Japan, took measures from the late 1960s to improve their management styles, productivity methods, and management-worker relations. In 1973 the government supported these trends by creating the National Agency for the Improvement of Work Conditions (ANACT). The lack of success of certain modern methods is that they appeared to the French as being imposed, rather than as being introduced by general consent, or as challenging individual autonomy. It was also argued that the focus on group work in pursuit of common goals weakens individual creativity. People would be reluctant to express dissent out of loyalty to the collectivity—a form of "groupthink" (Lebel, 1985, p. 27).

A modern French variant of participative management has been called consultation or dialogue (*la concertation*). More or less equal recognition is accorded both to the role of the group and the individual. Within small autonomous teams individuals keep their individuality rather than submerging their identity, since everyone is encouraged to contribute according to their abilities and experiences (Lebel, 1985, p. 44). Group leaders are respected because of their dynamism, their positions as partners rather than authority figures, and their capacity to adopt liberal attitudes toward subordinates (Exiga et al., 1981, p. 19; Sainsaulieu, 1987, p. 173). The glass company B.S.N. (Bousson-Souchon-Neuvecel) is an example of this management form.

The experience of one consultant is that many managers describe their style today as participative or institutional, but that subordinates rarely see their superiors' style in the same way. However, they prefer personally participative management. A study of the Center of Social Observation discovered that, while French employees are positively inclined toward participative management, they still wish to remain individualistic, having their own special results noticed and appreciated (Goguelin, 1989, p. 106).

STYLES OF HANDLING INTERPERSONAL CONFLICT

In French companies the distinction between interpersonal and intergroup conflicts is not always clear. A French employee who is involved in conflict situations with a superior, subordinates, or peers may wish to handle them on a person-to-person basis. However, the French often appeal for

outside support if they cannot obtain satisfaction from interpersonal negotiations. Workers might refer such matters to their peers, if they have strong
informal group affiliations, to their employee representatives (*les délégués
du personnel*), or to their union representative (*les délégués syndicaux*).

No one trade union has a monopoly in a French company, as in the
United States. The Auroux Laws of 1982 extended the powers of union representatives who could now negotiate directly with employers. If unionized workers have problems with a supervisor about work conditions, they
might refer the matter to their union representatives. The Auroux Laws
made collective negotiations obligatory between employers and workers.
The employee representative and the shop steward together usually act as
intermediaries, if requested, in dealing with an interpersonal conflict, or the
matter might result in direct management-union discussions. In any case,
interpersonal conflicts may spread (the contagion or displacement effect) if
the persons involved have strong group loyalties or duties.

Here are comments on five ways of handling interpersonal conflicts,
whether applied as an on-going process at work or to a particular formal
meeting or encounter.

Integrating

The French have traditionally not considered integrating as their first
strategy in interpersonal negotiations. However, since the late 1960s businesses have been encouraged both by outside forces, such as governments
or consultants, or by internal pressures to regard an integrating strategy as
a preferred option in most circumstances.

In frequent superior-subordinate conflicts since the early 1970s, where
the subordinate makes unpopular demands, likely to be awkward or
costly, and is in a powerful position, the superior will start with integrating, compromising being the fall-back option. Superiors are extremely reluctant to submit, to be the loser, if subordinates initially adopt dominating
strategies (Fauvet, 1974, p. 111). With peers a common first strategy of
managers and supervisors is generally integrating, with avoidance
adopted as a second option (Lebel, 1985, p. 155).

Managers and supervisors have increasingly handled problems with
subordinates on a nonconflictual basis before they became serious. This
form of conflict prevention has been reinforced by the application of well-
known repair strategies such as trying to identify the real source of a conflict, and at seeing a problem from the other person's viewpoint (role
reversal). The prime aim is to prevent an individual conflict escalating to
the group level or becoming polarized along the dimension separating
managers and supervisors (called *l'encadrement*) from the workers.

An example of conflict prevention is the evaluation meeting (*l'entretien
d'évaluation*), introduced in many larger French companies from the early

1980s, and largely confined to managerial levels. Each individual has an annual meeting with his or her immediate superior to discuss differences and to investigate how they can work together more effectively, particularly on new objectives.

One drawback the French see in the integrating approach is that cooperative solutions might sometimes be a false or artificial situation, if one side has cleverly manipulated the other. In addition, some regard the integrating outcome as an impossible state of unanimity or uniformity, which in the long run might lead to a weakening of the organization that encourages this process. Consequently, the French tend to stress integrating more as an approach to negotiations akin to the communicative/dialogue style (*la concertation*), rather than as an outcome.

The little-used French word *concertation* suddenly became fashionable after the Paris disturbances of 1968. The term has been applied broadly both to ways of negotiating or handling conflicts and to the consultative style of management. The word—close in meaning to integration—implies two parties working together jointly as allies or friendly colleagues rather than as rivals or competitors to solve common problems amicably.

Within industry, dialogue or concertation grew in importance from the early 1970s as a form of interpersonal negotiation. This approach originated largely in the informal or organic element of French structures, and focuses on the personal or affective aspect of the negotiating process. In addition, it includes an older French tradition—a sense of moderation that enables people to work together while agreeing to disagree (d'Iribarne, 1989, pp. 60–61). In other words, a successful outcome of dialogue can best be described as consensus (a popular French aim in meetings). This broad concept indicates that each party accepts the final decision, with various degrees of enthusiasm or resignation, which in practice could cover any of the five style options, but particularly integrating, compromising, avoiding, or accommodating.

Dialogue recognizes the importance of mutual face-saving. The French respect differences and the right to make mistakes. Even if integrating is the *process*, the party that realizes its position is weak may accept an *outcome* involving losing or accommodating. What is essential is that the side with the upper hand allows the conceding side to retain self-respect (other face maintenance). In addition both will participate equally in determining the outcome, which both consider is in the best interests of their organizations, is a fair result, or one serving the real interests of both parties.

Obliging

In theory this technique is not popular because the French rather dislike conceding points or admitting error, but in practice obliging is quite common as a means of improving management-worker relations. Much depends on what is at stake. If the matter is inconsequential a supervisor may accede to a subordinate's requirements, especially if the superior is on unsure ground or unable to count on his or her own boss for support. If someone becomes accommodating too early in some conflicts this may be seen as weakness, leading to the other party hardening its position.

Sometimes obliging is used as a long-term strategy in relations between peers or between superior and subordinate. One side makes greater concessions on this occasion, hoping the other will reciprocate accordingly later. An example is in the case of extra, unofficial holidays during the year (called bridges, *les ponts*). These tend to be a Friday or Monday so that when a religious holiday falls on a Thursday or Tuesday, it is customary to take the day after or preceding so as to lengthen the weekends.

Both sides usually assess the strengths, weaknesses, and power or "clout" of the other when negotiating. If both sides employ threats to be used if the other does not concede, it might be found that A is a little more powerful than B, but could also be harmed by B. Consequently, obliging might be the best policy in the circumstances.

Dominating

This forcing strategy has been the chief first option of superiors in companies with traditional management styles or organizational structures up until the late 1960s. Since then it has been more often a second or third option. However, it is still likely to be applied by superiors in discussions with subordinates in a critical situation when, for example, speedy or unpopular measures are imperative. This style is also important in companies or in particular departments or sections where dependency characterizes the relationship between subordinate and superior. This atmosphere is not conducive to problems being handled by genuine two-way communication, but rather by the superior trying to impose a solution (dominating) with the subordinate inevitably abandoning his or her initial position.

French managers and supervisors sometimes devise special tactics for winning when in conflict with their subordinates. One is to give a subordinate a difficult project. When he or she fails the subordinate may lose self-confidence, and become more dependent on the superior. Another is to divert a conflict a superior may have with two subordinates by getting the latter to compete with each other rather than challenging his or her authority. This is done by giving them identical tasks. In the case of the manager really obsessed by power-seeking, the narcissist, then a pseudo-cooperative style may be practiced to hide the preferred style-dominating (Lebel, 1985, p. 113).

Since the late 1960s individual employees have been far less likely to acquiesce in dominating strategies applied by superiors. However, subordinates may have no choice but to submit if they work in certain low pay jobs such as catering, dry-cleaning, and the clothing industry. Managers are by no means alone in the importance they attribute to using power to influence relationships and in handling conflicts and negotiations. Workers who do adopt dominating strategies with superiors recognize the need for having more persuasive threats or sanctions than their superiors. At work a subordinate might threaten to take a matter up with the union or the *prud'homme* (see section on "Alternative Dispute Management") if unable to get satisfaction from his or her superior.

While autocratic managers may remain fairly firm or dominating in negotiations with subordinates regarding aims and distribution of work, they are more flexible or accommodating today regarding methods by which objectives are achieved.

Avoiding

This technique is viewed more positively by theorists and negotiators in France than in the United States. The French take a longer time perspective than Anglo-Saxons, who are often anxious to deal with problems and decision-taking matters fairly quickly. In contrast, French managers tend to be perfectionists and dislike making errors. Consequently a manager may avoid handling a conflict firmly, pleading lack of time or insufficiency of information. By delaying in taking any positive action or intervening, the manager may hope the problem will eventually disappear.

Although avoiding tended to be a second option to dominating, in certain situations it became the first strategy. Paternalist managers used to regard negotiations with subordinates as superfluous, based on the belief that they understood the needs and problems of employees better than the latter did. This style of nonnegotiation has been described as both identification and avoidance (Lebel, 1985, p. 156).

Many French managers still instinctively dislike conflict situations at work, whether with superiors, subordinates, or peers. Managers, particularly those associated with paternalist or "country club" leadership styles who try to create a togetherness atmosphere, may refuse to admit that a real conflict exists or try to smooth over differences. They may try to avoid conflict by making additional complimentary remarks to subordinates or divert attention from disagreement by changing the subject. If a problem is raised the manager may reply with comments such as "I don't want to know about it." This is a means of stifling conflicts used by superiors who surround themselves by "yes men."

One variation of the avoiding strategy is shifting the responsibility to someone else. This is commonly done in France if a person is in an intermediary position, and when not too much difference exists in rank. A laissez-faire manager or supervisor, in particular, fond of delegating, may abandon a conflict with comments such as "Do it your way!"

Other ploys are promising to do something about a complaint, then doing nothing; or proposing an ambiguous solution that allows both sides to feel they have gained something, which in reality is a false compromise as well as an escape from the problem. Sometimes people try to avoid involvement in a conflict of others (a triad), arguing that it is not their affair, or that they are unwilling to stir things up (*pas de vagues*). A classic situation is where the personnel director is caught in a dispute between the union representative and the chief executive. One common French practice, if one or both sides feel that their aims are irreconcilable, is to break off relations—a separation (*une cassure*) (Fauvet, 1974, p. 83).

A superior at work today may adopt avoidance at the official level, perhaps hoping pressing problems will resolve themselves or be sorted out informally rather than by a face-to-face encounter. This approach is described by one manager as "better to do nothing than disappoint" (Barsoux & Lawrence, 1990, p. 113).

Avoidance for many French is not only a negotiation option, but a general norm of behavior adopted toward others outside the circle of family and close friends. The French desire for independence and autonomy often leads to a restriction of direct encounters both at and outside work. The continued adherence of many French to systematic structures is quite logical, considering such organizations aim to make conflict unnecessary. So much is worked out in advance what everyone has to do, so there should be less need for people to discuss with others what is required (Gruère & Morel, 1991, p. 12). If subordinates make mistakes, superiors may adopt an avoidance attitude ("I don't want to be involved") based on the principle of leaving them to deal with minor problems.

Compromising

Anglo-Saxons tend to have a positive image of this technique, and assume that compromising or integrating are the best strategies in the long term on important matters. The French do not have the English notion of fair play, and compromise is often regarded as a second-best solution associated with weakness. A sound, logical, carefully thought-out position should not be abandoned unless the reasoning is wrong.

The habit of making mutual concessions through bargaining may be interpreted negatively as *une compromission,* a shady deal, dishonesty, or opportunism, or as something phony or faulty (*un compromis boiteux*). In other words, a disagreement may continue in a disguised or latent form, although for official purposes two powerful departmental heads appear to have found a satisfactory arrangement (Fauvet, 1974, pp. 83, 162). Alternatively, a form of negative cooperation occurs when parties (possibly superior-subordinate) agree to disagree (a compromise arrangement) and continue working together. In practice the French do make compromises but prefer terms such as "consensus" to describe this process when negotiating.

ALTERNATIVE DISPUTE MANAGEMENT

When an employer and workers or trade union representatives used to meet for negotiations, neither searched in reality for positive creative solutions. Negotiation itself was seen as a competitive power struggle (*rapport de force*), where each side tried to make its own views prevail, while adopting a defensive position toward opposing arguments. Both concealed important information and developed a strategy for identifying and controlling areas of uncertainty within the dialogue, parallel to the attempts of fencing partners to find weaknesses in the swordsmanship of their adversaries (Lebel, 1985, p. 113).

In view of what has been said above, it was not surprising that since the 1930s the state has traditionally acted as a major partner with industry, helping large firms cope with major crises (Sainsaulieu, 1987, p. 160). Government help in resolving major disputes has sometimes occurred following the requests of the employers or the unions, or when the government itself decides to intervene.

If senior management encounters a serious problem at work, the chief executive might resort to his or her network of contacts in the civil service or government for advice and help. Often the heads of major organizations are chosen partly for their "outside influence." Leading or important civil servants, politicians, and businesspeople tend to share a common background and outlook toward many issues based on having been educated at one of the leading and more exclusive of the Grandes Ecoles. The training received in these higher educational institutions (considered more prestigious than universities) is sufficiently broad to allow the very able to rise to the top whether in the public or private sector. As a result, a lasting web of interlocking formal and informal links unite former alumni of these schools, one factor contributing to close business-government relations in France.

Disregarding possible resort to direct state intervention, the major forms of alternative dispute management techniques have been conciliation and mediation, sometimes supported by quasi-official support from the Ministry of Labor and the courts. The Confédération Francaise du Travail (CFDT) is the only major union to support conciliation and mediation procedures. The Force Ouvrière is the most moderate of the major unions, and supports direct management-worker negotiations rather than direct state intervention.

The best-known conciliatory procedures are the *conseils de prud'hommes*, locally elected committees comprising two people. One represents the employers (*les patrons*) and the other the employees. Trade unions usually have sizable influence in the selection of the latter. These small committees, elected for six years, are chosen for each branch of industrial activity. Their object is to achieve cordial settlements or a consensus among the interested parties (*l'arrangement a l'amiable*). The *conseils de prud'hommes* meet monthly and deal with individual work contracts, accidents, sickness, cases where people have temporarily or permanently become unemployed, and procedural reforms. If either of the parties is dissatisfied with the outcome, they can appeal to the Court of Appeal for a judicial ruling.

In the event of major disputes in companies, between employers, workers, and their unions, conciliation has been little used as a method of resolving conflicts since the government first instituted conciliatory procedures in 1950 (Touzard, 1977, p. 104). One notable success, however, was in the case of a strike of the Peugeot company workers at Sochaux and Mulhouse in 1988. The Ministry of Labor appointed a conciliator, who managed to get the employers and trade unions to agree on a settlement.

Work inspectors from the Ministry of Labor visit businesses on a regular basis to ensure that the laws are respected. The distinction between conciliation and mediation is not always clear-cut and sometimes work inspectors unofficially visit companies, if required, to carry out informal mediation or conciliation regarding disputes between employers and employees. They will size up the situation (*tâter le terrain*) during a visit, gather all necessary information, and give appropriate advice if tension is high or something critical has occurred that might lead to a major conflict. In this respect, they help to prevent conflict. In some cases work inspectors have been successful in helping resolve work conflicts. If a worker complains about a delicate matter concerning security, health, or accident risks, the supervisor might refer the matter directly to a work inspector.

A series of laws since 1955 have aimed at encouraging businesses to use mediation procedures as an alternative to conciliation or arbitration. Conciliation was little used, while arbitration involved costly delays. Mediation has been successfully applied in many areas outside industrial relations, including cases involving public authorities and private citizens. Official recognition of the importance of mediation is reflected in the appointment of a national mediator in 1973, the equivalent of the ombudsman in Britain, officially called *Le Médiateur de la République*. Major towns, including Paris, also have an official mediator now.

Mediation in the industrial field following procedures recognized in the Code of Work (Code de Travail) has not developed much since the 1950s. Only 168 cases were mediated between 1955 and 1964. Between 1975 and 1985 fourteen mediations took place nationally, eight being concluded successfully, while eleven out of the thirty-four regional mediations succeeded (Six, 1990, p. 120). However, work inspectors have been successful, unofficially, in helping find amicable solutions to work conflicts. In critical situations businesses can appeal to the courts who can appoint mediators.

Official mediation has not been popular either with business leaders or trade unionists. Often when unionists have requested external intervention, employers have seen this as a form of pressure. Agreement of both parties is required before a mediator is chosen. The state, in default of such agreement, can choose a mediator from a list of competent people held by the Ministry of Works. Such people are normally not specifically trained mediators but experienced businesspeople or senior civil servants (Touzard, 1977, p. 157).

In recent years judicial mediation has developed with judges designating mediators to resolve major conflicts, as in the case of the aeronautical company SNECMA. Jurists are by no means in agreement as to whether this new departure is likely to succeed in the long term.

Unofficial or private mediation has progressed in the last ten years. One reason has been the desire of employers to solve internal problems without the involvement of trade union representatives. The Centre National de la Mediation has a branch that provides training for mediators. Consultancy firms or individual consultants are sometimes invited by employers to advise on certain problems. Often these outsiders act in the role of mediators or use their skills in the field of conflict prevention, helping businesses to use human resources more effectively or to improve internal communications.

DISCUSSION

Various writers have highlighted the contradictory or paradoxical aspects of the French and their culture. An aspect of this is reflected in the midpoint position where France has been placed on the systematic-organic dimension (Mole, 1990, p. 188). This can be interpreted not as indicating French indifference or moderateness in relation to these ideas, but rather the tendency to oscillate between the extremes of both. Another aspect is that the highly individualistic French also exhibit features more commonly found in collectivist cultures, such as social focus on family, consensus, people relationships, and even on organic or informal practices.

The opposing tendencies outlined above are reflected in the French approach to conflict management. Although well-developed institutional procedures exist in French companies for regulating conflicts, there is a tendency to settle internal conflicts unofficially, those involved devising their own informal techniques and solutions that might best be described under concepts such as personalism (degree to which people interact personally), consensus, concertation (dialogue), or *l'accord á l'amiable* (friendly agreement). Between them these broad concepts cover all five styles of negotiation and other approaches, the latter close to but not identical with any of the five styles.

In 1978 the government tried in vain by law to introduce concertation into business as a modus vivendi for operations. Basically it involves various repair strategies for breaking deadlocks in a conciliatory manner, as developed by practitioners, mediators, and scholars in the field of conflict, peace-building, or within and outside industry both in France and elsewhere.

The French have been reputed for their fascination with elegant grand schemes rather than for mundane feasible projects. Their tendency individually at work to sometimes modify the orders or designs of others to demonstrate their own involvement in the course of events or creativity is echoed in academic works. Specialist writers on conflict are frequently appreciated who develop on a logical basis their own models, techniques, and practices rather than merely working within the confines of existing theories already known internationally (Goguelin, 1989, p. 148).

Francois de Callières, a French diplomat, wrote the first book on negotiation in 1716. He discussed the basic dilemmas as to whether negotiators should adopt a fighting or a cooperative approach, and also whether they should add a third option of avoidance, evasion or delay, when the negotiators refuse to reveal their position. Since then writers on negotiating theory have developed two-, three-, four-, and five-style models they feel best fit reality. It is up to the practitioner and researcher in each country or society to ascertain what model best fits the methods commonly used in that culture.

The advantage of the Rahim Organizational Conflict Inventory–II (ROCI–II) is that it assumes a broader framework than the others, a five-style model from which information can be obtained as to which of five options, including dominating (fighting) or integrating (cooperating), are predominant in certain cultures under various circumstances. Based on my own research and impressions, and the findings of writers on French ways of handling conflict and negotiating, there seems to be a preference for broadly two- or three-style models, based either on the pair dominating-integrating or the trio dominating-integrating-avoiding.

This study of French conflict-handling styles gives rise to certain points that may help future researchers:

1. Research could be carried out both within major businesses and among French politicians and diplomats active in conflict management so as to ascertain the particular styles that tend to predominate, and how options or strategies used are labeled.

2. Questionnaires such as the ROCI–II need to be supplemented by open-ended questions that require participants to describe their own preferred negotiating style, after they have been informed what the five-style approach entails. This will help unearth other possible worthwhile styles.

3. The same research project should be carried out in similar organizations in various parts of a country to discover whether regional cultural

differences affected the results. Results are likely to vary concerning conflict-handling techniques, for example, between Lorraine (eastern France
close to Germany, a strongly systematic culture) and southern France
(close to Italy and Spain, both organic-tending cultures).

ACKNOWLEDGMENTS

The author would like to acknowledge the help with resources and advice provided by Jacques Salzer (University of Paris IX–Dauphine), Hubert
Touzard (University of Paris V–René Descartes), and Alexis Kurc (University of Nancy II).

REFERENCES

Barsoux, J.-L., & Lawrence, P. (1990). *Management in France.* London: Cassell.
Blake, R. R., & Mouton, J. S. (1985). *The managerial grid III.* Houston: Gulf.
Comp-Langlois, H. (1984). Le management paradoxal: Une theorie Française du
    management [Paradoxical management: A French theory of management].
    Revue Française de Gestion, No. 47, 123–124.
d'Iribarne, P. (1989). *La logigue de l'honneur* [The logic of principle]. Paris: Seuil.
Exiga, A., Piotet, F., & Sainsaulieu, R. (1981). *L'analyse sociologique des conditions de
    travail* [A sociological analysis of work conditions]. Paris: Agence Nationale
    pour l'Amelioration des Conditions de Travail.
Fauvet, J. C. (1974). *Comprendre les conflits sociaux* [Understanding social conflicts].
    Paris: Les Editions D'organization.
Goguelin, P. (1989). *Le management psychologique des organizations* [Psychological as-
    pects of managing organizations] (Vol.2.) Paris: Esfetiteur.
Gruère, J. P., & Morel, P. (1991). *Cadres Français et communications interculturelles*
    [French managers and intercultural communication]. Paris: Eyrolles.
Hall, E. T., & Hall, M. R. (1990). *Understanding cultural differences.* Yarmouth, ME:
    Intercultural Press.
Hofstede, G. (1991). *Cultures and organizations.* London: McGraw-Hill.
Laurent, A. (1986). The cross-cultural puzzle of international human resource man-
    agement. *Human Resources Management* 25 (1), 91–102.
Lebel, P. (1985). *Le triangle du manaqement* [The management triangle]. Paris: Les
    Editions D'organization.
Lee, H. O., & Rogan, R. G. (1991). A cross-cultural comparison of organizational
    conflict management behaviors. *International Journal of Conflict Management,*
    2, 181–199.
Linhart, D. (1990). Quels changements dans l'entreprise? [What changes in busi-
    ness?]. *Reseaux—Communication, Technologie, Societe.* No. 41.
Mole, J. (1990). *Mind your manners.* London: The Industrial Society.
Sainsaulieu, R. (1987). *Sociologie de l'organization et de l'entreprise* [Sociological as-
    pects of organization and business]. Paris: Dalloz.
Six, J. F. (1990). *Le temps des mediateurs* [The hour of mediators]. Paris: Seuil.

Ting-Toomey, S., Gao, G., Trubisky, P., Yang, Z., Kim, H. S., Lin, S.-L., & Nishida, T. (1991). Culture, face maintenance, and styles of handling interpersonal conflict : A study in five cultures. *International Journal of Conflict Management, 2,* 275–296.

Touzard, H. (1977). *La mediation et la resolution des conflits* [Mediation and conflict resolution]. Paris: PUF.

Vachette, J. L. (1984). Le modèle Français du changement [The French model of change]. *Revue Française de gestion,* No. 47, 119–122.

3

JAPAN

Robert T. Moran, Jonathan Allen, Richard Wichmann, Tomoko Ando, and Machiko Sasano

This chapter delineates the Japanese cultural approaches to conflict management and negotiations. It is designed to provide a basic foundation for understanding conflict management in the hope of assisting in the development of a new effective model for intercultural conflict management and negotiation with the Japanese.

A new global economic power equilibrium and restructured international political relationships have resulted from this advent of the Japanese into the international community, demanding increased contact and exposure between Japan and the Western world. Enshrouding this increased intercultural communication has been a blanket of misunderstanding, confusion, and cross-cultural ignorance that has brought about much friction, stress, and anger by businesspeople and political leaders on both sides of the Pacific. The unfavorable results of these cross-cultural endeavors underscore the need for a new international conflict management system, one that is culturally oriented and rooted firmly in a thorough understanding of the nature and internal conflict management system utilized within Japanese society.

Over the last two decades Japan has emerged on the international stage as a major world actor. Propelling Japan's arrival as a new world superpower has been its dynamic, expanding economy, which has thrust the traditionally insular nation of Asia into the heart of the global economic marketplace and international political arena. As a major player in the world scene, conflicts with collaborators and competitors are inevitable. This chapter delineates the Japanese cultural approaches to conflict management.

To understand typical behavioral responses to conflict situations in Japan, however, requires a basic understanding of the history and cultural environment of Japan. Accordingly, it is necessary to first ascertain the key psychological and cultural variables that affect Japanese conflict management phenomena, and then to determine how they interrelate with each other to create various deviations within a larger cultural norm. An investigation into the cultural context of Japan provides the Western observer with an understanding of and appreciation for the distinct nature and form of conflict management within Japanese society.

To properly compare conflict management in Japan with that experienced in other cultural settings, however, involves far more than mere understanding of the fact that the Japanese culture is different. One of the critical mistakes that a neophyte to the international world can make in such a cross-cultural comparison is that of extrapolating one's native conflict situations into another's cultural framework. Not only are the cultures different, but also the behavioral and conflict phenomena, as well as the behavioral alternatives available to members of the respective culture. In relation to a cross-cultural comparison of conflict management, the essential question for the Western observer is not how the Japanese manage, in their own cultural setting, conflicts familiar to the Western observer. Rather, the focus must be to determine the types of conflicts the Japanese experience, and the cultural restraints and behavioral techniques they use to manage their conflicts, given their own culturally acceptable set of alternatives. Many of the conflict situations considered in the Western world representing major sources of interpersonal and organizational conflict seldom exist in the Japanese organizational model.

The Japanese conflict management system includes both institutionalized conflict management structures and behavioral conflict management techniques. Approaching the topic from an intracultural standpoint will allow the reader to circumvent the temptation to begin comparing conflicts, and will aid in placing the focus instead upon the techniques and methods employed by the Japanese in the management of their own native conflicts. Then and only then is it possible to begin to make an effective comparison of the conflict management techniques utilized in different cultural settings.

It is important to keep in mind throughout this chapter that the material presented is based upon the Japan of yesterday and today. The Japan of tomorrow will surely be very different, because Japan is currently undergoing one of the greatest cultural evolutions in its history. Since its entrance in the last two decades into the international community as a global economic and political power, Japan has been forced to shake off its historical insularity and to open itself to foreign ideas and influences. The resulting social and psychological impacts resulting from this exposure are transforming Japanese society, seemingly overnight, from the bottom up. The new generation in Japan is a completely different breed of Japanese, and the Japan in which they will work and live will no doubt become foreign to the older generation. Despite the changes, many deep-rooted cultural traits, values, and practices will continue to shape the Japan of the future. It is these distinctly Japanese cultural variables that will be highlighted as they pertain to the topic of conflict management.

SOCIAL, CULTURAL, AND ECONOMIC FACTORS

The roots of Japanese conflict management have evolved through its long rich history. The closely tied, homogeneous society has an altogether different view of and approach to conflict than that found in Western cultures. Beginning in the Tokugawa Shogunate of the sixteenth century, Confucian values, such as harmony and a need for order and unity, were deeply implanted into Japanese consciousness. Later, toward the end of the nineteenth century when Japan was finally opened to the Western world, the Meiji leaders continued to strengthen a world view and to establish it as a cornerstone of Japanese tradition. National unity and selfless devotion to the collective good became even more explicit, and consequently were permanently inculcated into the societal fabric.

A linguistic survey of the concepts associated with conflict sheds some additional light on the Japanese perspective. Here are several Japanese words with short descriptions of their meaning as possible translations of "conflict":

toosoo	war, fight
arasoi	a strong word meaning small war
ototsu	collision, clash
masatsu	friction
kattou	trouble, complications, struggle
fuicchi, fuchowa	disharmony

A direct translation of conflict is not easily obtainable, for it encompasses a wide range of concepts from "war" and "fight" on one end of the semantic continuum to "disharmony" and "friction" on the other end. Despite the semantic variation utilized in a given conversational setting, the elements of incompatibility and disagreement are almost always present.

The Japanese, as do all people, experience conflict and disagreements. However, they accomplish resolution by implicitly solving the conflict, if possible by saving face, depersonalizing the conflict, or by using a third party to mediate between those involved. A recent study by Cosier et al. (1992) considers the cooperation and conflict that may occur in *ura* (the informal arena) in Japanese conflict resolution and decision-making.

Hofstede (1980) in his book *Culture's Consequences* identifies four dimensions of national culture, which suggest that a worldwide learning of U.S.

concepts of leadership may be impossible. These cultural dimensions are power distance, uncertainty avoidance, individualism/collectivism, and masculinity/femininity. Power distance indicates the extent to which a society accepts that power in institutions and organizations is distributed unequally. Uncertainty avoidance indicates the extent to which a society feels threatened by an uncertain or ambiguous situation. Individualism refers to a loosely knit social framework in a society in which people are supposed to take care of themselves and of their immediate families only. Ting-Toomey et al. (1991) note that individualism/collectivism does not only apply to national cultures but also to ethnic groups in that national culture. First-generation Asian-Americans tend to keep their group-oriented values; European-Americans tend to retain their individualistic orientation. Collectivism, the opposite, occurs when there is a tight social framework in which people distinguish between in-groups and out-groups; they expect their in-group (relatives, clan, organizations) to look after them, and in exchange for that owe absolute loyalty to it. The fourth dimension is masculinity with its opposite pole, femininity. This dimension expresses the extent to which the dominant values in society are assertiveness, money and things, not caring for others, quality of life, and people.

In Hofstede's most recent book, *Cultures and Organizations* (1991), fifty countries and three regions reflective of each dimension are cited. On the power distance index, Japan ranked thirty-three and the United States was thirty-eight. On the individualism index, Japan ranked twenty-two and the United States was first. On the masculinity index, Japan was first and the United States ranked fifteen and on the uncertainty avoidance, Japan was seven and the United States was forty-three.

The consequences of Hofstede's conclusion are significant. Strategies to manage conflict are learned and are based on assumptions about one's place in the world. Like leadership and power, conflict is a fascinating subject for research and discussion in organizations and family systems. Traditionally, the social scientists who have studied conflict have been keenly aware of its destructive element, which was observed in wars, strikes, family disruption, and disharmony whenever a conflict was observed. But in the past two or three decades the idea that conflict is only destructive and is therefore to be avoided at all costs has been replaced with the reality that conflict is present in most organizations and institutions and, if managed well, serves useful purposes. As Likert and Likert (1976) have stated, the strategies and principles used by a society in dealing with disagreements reflect the basic values and philosophy in that society.

Even though there may be differences of opinion, the Japanese will not make it obvious to one another. Japan is a high-context society in which communication between people is not achieved primarily through the words they use, but rather through the high degree of nonverbal signals given in the context of their communication. The great sensitivity of Japanese to linguistic and behavioral cues that indicate dissatisfaction is a crucial part of their communication system. Direct confrontation is culturally unacceptable. Very rarely will a Japanese individual enter willingly into an argument. Instead, he or she will convert the external conflict into an internal psychological or emotional one, internalizing his or her emotions in the process. As a result, the external conflict will dissipate without any confrontation or discussion of the conflict taking place. In this way, harmony has been preserved and no one has lost face.

The Japanese word *wa* is usually translated into English as "harmony," but in Japanese society *wa* connotes consensus, or the absence of conflict, *and* is valued very highly. It is so important to reach agreement within a group that conflicts are almost always shunned or denied, but rarely solved. Therefore, the Japanese do not usually argue or debate, since arguing is associated with conflict.

Japanese conflict dynamics are also quite different from those in the West. For conflict to occur in Japan, people must be at the same organizational or social level, as between co-workers or between supervisors. Conflict very rarely occurs between individuals of dissimilar levels, as between an employee and his or her supervisor. For the most part, subordinates are prevented from showing or expressing their discontent or disagreement with their supervisors because of stringent social protocol.

It is difficult and misleading to analyze Japanese organizations outside of their cultural context. Perhaps it is the superficial similarities that modern business institutions around the world share that cause the Western observer to overlook the more significant differences. However, an anthropological perspective, which emphasizes the cultural factors at play within organizational settings, offers many insights into the inner workings of Japanese organizations, and will therefore be emphasized throughout this chapter.

A very prominent feature of the Japanese cultural fabric is its high degree of conformity. This strong cultural trait of conformity is referred to as *uchi/soto* dichotomy. At all levels of Japanese society, one's identity and place within the social and economic structure is largely dependent upon the groups to which one belongs. This group predisposition is encouraged by a world view that places very high emphasis upon "insiders" and "outsiders," reflected by the Japanese words *uchi* and *soto*, respectively. This *uchi/soto* concept is very prominent in the Japanese consciousness of human relationships. They draw distinct lines between "us" and "them" and have developed a semiotic system within the group. Members of the group maintain a common sense of identity and solidarity that cannot be shared by out-group members.

Within the group, members feel responsibility for each other's actions. This distinction between *uchi* and *soto* is socially approved. Group ties are so strong that members develop feelings almost like those experienced in a family. The idea that all members of the company share a common fate, or are "riding in the same boat," is emphasized. A Japanese company is often referred to as "one great family." The boundary between company life and home life is not well defined, as the employee's entire life revolves around the company. It is quite natural, then, to think of one's working colleagues as members of a large family.

The Japanese may appear to be the rudest or the most polite people, depending on whether they are dealing with in-group members or out-group members. A person might be very polite and pleasant to other individuals within one's inner circle, but will behave with complete indifference toward out-group members who have no connection.

Anthropologist Ruth Benedict indicated in her book *The Chrysanthemum and the Sword* (1954) that Japan is a shame culture as opposed to Western guilt cultures. Shame plays an important role in Japanese conduct and morality, because the Japanese are socialized to be very sensitive to the opinions and feelings of others. The Japanese are extremely afraid of betraying the trust of members in their own group. If they do so, they have been conditioned socially to experience a great sense of shame, which is the strongest Japanese psychological sanction.

In Japan, a sense of shame is a function of human relations. The Japanese feel shame when they have a falling out with their own group, or are out of step with the group. In this context, a sense of shame and a sense of fear are very closely linked. In general, the Japanese are keenly aware of how things should be handled and how they are expected to behave in different circumstances. As a result, they feel extremely uncomfortable when things are not the way they should be, and will try to prevent uncertainty as much as possible. Communication patterns between Japanese are such that they provide constant reassurance in social life. Because of their fear of not living up to social expectations, the Japanese can be very inflexible when dealing with things that do not fit neatly into their existing cultural patterns.

There is a Japanese proverb that says, "The traveler discards his sense of shame." People who usually behave reasonably in their home town behave just as they please once they are away from home. At home, however, the Japanese are vulnerable to the threat of shame within the group and are psychologically paralyzed by the thought of being expelled socially from the group, so they must behave with other members in their inner circle in a manner that is harmonious and orderly. This provides no opportunity for the risk of intragroup conflict.

Another reason for the high degree of conformity within Japanese society is the extensive homogeneity of its people. Primarily due to the historical, geographic, and political insularity of Japan, it has been able to retain a relatively high degree of ethnic, linguistic, religious, and cultural homogeneity. More important has been the impact this homogeneity has had on the values of the people, and on the ability of government and industry to harness this homogeneity and focus it toward common objectives and goals with little resistance from the public. Understood in this context, the so-called Japanese Economic Miracle is more axiomatic than miraculous. Once the national will was in place, the objectives could be reached without any of the social inefficiencies that result from competing values, interests, and goals inherent in a pluralistic society.

MANAGERIAL STYLES

From a conflict-management standpoint, Japan presents a relatively clear example of a country in which two major conflict-management styles are used: obliging and avoiding. The similarity of the two styles rests in the fact that concern for self is almost always subjugated in conflict situations, often associated with a cultural priority to avoid recognition of a dispute or confrontation.

Conflict management in Japan is regulated primarily through two major societal vehicles: institutional structures and behavioral conflict management techniques. The institutional channel is addressed first, since it restricts most of the potential conflict within Japanese organizations.

One of the greatest differences between American firms and Japanese firms is the nature of the employer's relationship to employees. In an American context, such a relationship is often perceived as being adversarial in nature. The concept is fundamentally grounded in a capitalistic interpretation of employment, in which parties with competing interests find a value of exchange of labor for wages, which is determined primarily by labor market forces. Under such a system, both employer and employee seek to maximize their own welfare through exploitation of any opportunities that may arise that allow them to gain relative to the other party. Accordingly, in such a market-oriented approach to employment, the nature of the relationship between employee and employer exists so long as parties have no better economic alternatives. Loyalty in such a context, then, is merely the respective intersection between the employer's and employee's alternatives.

Such a cold market approach to employment by the Japanese is prevented by certain attitudes and systems established within the organizational culture. The most important of these is the lifetime employment system. In Japanese industry, once an employee joins a company, he or she is guaranteed employment until retirement, unless the employee chooses to leave the company for some reason. The ramifications of such a system extend far beyond the employee/employer relationship, providing an organizational structure in which the existence and degree of conflict is greatly minimized. The risks inherent in the employee/employer relationship are also reduced, since each party is relatively assured of a "lifelong" relationship. The decision to invest time, training, and company resources into the employee is almost an automatic one, with the degree of investment limited only by the company resources available. Cross-training is viewed as a corporate developmental measure rather than an employee privilege. Inefficiencies resulting from constant turnover and its related retraining are nonexistent.

One of the key pillars of the lifetime employment concept is the way in which the Japanese view their organization. In Japan companies are managed as a "community," in contrast to those in many Western countries in which they are managed as an economic organization.

In the West, companies are mainly places where employees earn money to live. For Japanese workers, their companies are viewed as communities as well as workplaces. In Japan, once an individual embarks upon a career, the role of close friends, who studied and socialized together at the university, is replaced by working colleagues. The Japanese spend a great deal of time with their colleagues after working hours, drinking at bars, playing golf, or even traveling and vacationing together. While it might be difficult for Americans or Europeans to understand why the Japanese can enjoy their free time with colleagues, who are viewed as competitors, it is not difficult for the Japanese, because their companies are run like well-managed communities where people develop very strong personal ties.

Many of the unwritten rules of Japanese social life have been transferred into companies' management systems. Some of the most important rules of Japanese community life, avoiding conflict at all costs and maintaining harmony among group members, provide the basis for the Japanese management system. One unique aspect of Japanese conflict management is that the management system works to prevent conflicts or to fail to acknowledge them, rather than to actually resolve any conflicts that have already been generated. Rooted deeply in the Japanese cultural environment, several unique institutionalized conflict management schemes were developed to minimize the interpersonal conflict in Japanese organizational life: the seniority system, *dohki* groups, and the *ringi* system.

The seniority system is essentially a payment and promotion system based upon the time an individual has worked for a company. This system works smoothly within the lifetime employment environment. This system developed after World War I as a rational response to the scarcity of well-trained labor for more demanding technical jobs. The manufacturers guaranteed workers job security and wage increases in order to entice them to join the firm. It should be noted that under the lifetime employment system, generally speaking, there is an almost perfect correlation between seniority and the age of the employee. Although this system grew out of a need for a strong labor pool, it is supported by and fits well into Japanese culture, which emphasizes respect for older people, a strong work ethic, and group attitudes.

This seniority system produces a number of significant side benefits, one of which is the reduction of conflict between superiors and subordinates. Under the well-developed seniority system, employees are not only compensated but also promoted based on their seniority. Younger employees know that they will never surpass their superiors, even if they are more capable. Although from a Western viewpoint this might seem to be an ineffective and unfair policy, especially for capable young people, this system eliminates any sense of competition and conflict across age or status lines. Those higher on the career "escalator" are seen merely as older persons who got on the escalator earlier.

The seniority system is composed of many strata of age or peer groups known as *dohki* groups. A *dohki* group consists of all the employees who began their careers with the company during a given year, and represents a type of peer group that facilitates the management of conflict in Japanese organizations. *Dohki* groups also play an important social role as formal and informal organizations within the large corporate structure. It should be noted that almost all Japanese college graduates are the same age and are hired by companies to start work at the same time soon after their college graduation. The newly hired employees attend the company's orientation and education programs together.

Under the seniority system, people in the same *dohki* group (a *dohki* group that started to work in 1980, for example, might be called 80-*dohki*) with the same level of education are compensated and even promoted together over the years as long as possible. Of course, in the future some of them will become executives and others will not, but at least during the first ten or fifteen years their titles and salaries will be almost equivalent. A strong sense of solidarity exists among people in the same *dohki* group. They treat each other like special friends rather than co-workers. They do not need to compete with each other and therefore are not concerned with their colleagues' salaries or perquisites. Under the seniority system, a member of a given *dohki* group will never be requested to work under another who belongs to the same *dohki* group. If an employee of the 80-*dohki* group is selected as a leader of a certain project team, other project members would be selected from younger *dohki* groups, such as from the 81- or 82-*dohki* group.

Some individuals wonder how Japanese companies can maintain the seniority system and *dohki* group parity in pyramid-shaped organizational structures. There are only a few positions of general management, and it is impossible to promote all *dohki* members at the same time. To solve this problem, many Japanese companies have created numerous "phantom" titles and positions, which often lead to very complicated and confusing organizational structures. For example, between a general manager and a product or line manager there might be an assistant to the general manager, an assistant general manager, and a deputy general manager. Sometimes it is even quite difficult for insiders to figure out what the difference is among these titles and their respective work responsibilities.

Japanese compensation arrangements parallel the *dohki* system in terms of their nature. When young graduates are hired by the company, they all receive the same compensation regardless of the educational institution that they attended or of their unique personal backgrounds. For the most part, all members of a given *dohki* will receive equal pay increases based upon a graduated pay scale. This pay scale system is directly linked to the slow but steady movement up the seniority escalator. This graduated pay-scale system can be contrasted to the so-called merit system practiced by many American firms. Superior performance and extraordinary ability are recognized in Japan, but seldom are financially and professionally compensated because of the stringent rules of the seniority system. The seniority of an employee plays the greatest role in the determination of an employee's compensation. In very few circumstances would the Japanese risk upsetting the traditional employment system to reward or promote an outstanding worker beyond the limits of the established seniority structure.

The organizational systems, which have been mentioned so far, give the impression that Japanese companies and society are rigidly organized without any flexibility. As a result, Japanese society is often referred to as a "vertical society." However, many kinds of informal organizations provide the Japanese with flexible communication networks in vertical and horizontal directions. These informal organizations play a vital role as organizational "lubricants" and are indispensable elements in the proper functioning of the community. In addition to the *dohki* groups, there are other informal organizations like alumni associations (usually only for college graduates), recreational groups, and various clubs.

Japanese, particularly those who graduated from a well-known traditional university, often strongly identify and associate themselves with their universities. Each *dohki* group and alumni association has its exclusive party once or twice a year to maintain the personal ties of its members. In most Japanese companies, there are also many kinds of club activities, such as tennis, skiing, and basketball. Many members of these clubs spend a lot of time together after working hours or on weekends and sometimes take short trips together on holidays without their spouses and children. Many companies have their own gymnasium, resort, or recreational facilities for their employees, and these informal organizational networks are encouraged by companies as effective tools to prevent interpersonal conflict among employees in the company. The personal networks established by these informal organizations are used as additional communication systems for the business.

The *ringi*-system is one in which co-workers informally circulate proposals in document form throughout the company prior to formal submission of a proposal. Members of the company affix their seals on the proposal as a sign that they have seen the document and will not later oppose the proposal when it is formally presented. This unique Japanese decision-making and conflict management system is often called "bottom-up decision-making," in contrast to top-down decision-making practiced in other cultures. This system makes it possible to gather support from lower levels in the organization before an upper-level decision is made. As characterized by this system in Japanese organizations, very careful and extensive consultations before actual decision-making are highly valued. Before the final decision is made, people have many formal and informal meetings (sometimes called *nemawashi*), and negotiations or consultations continue until general consensus is achieved, avoiding opinion clashes in the process if at all possible. Although Japanese decision-making is often criticized for the length of time required to reach decisions, the Japanese willingly spend the time to minimize conflicts that might arise later during the decision process.

The *ringi*-system is an indispensable process and necessary to achieve general consensus. A proposal is revised many times throughout the process until it is acceptable to everyone. Later, the final decision to accept the proposal is made in a formal meeting, but this meeting is nothing more than a ritual rubber-stamping procedure, which is performed to confirm the decision that was already informally reached. The *ringi* system not only helps to avoid open confrontation, but it also disperses responsibility throughout the entire hierarchy. Even if the decision later proved to be a poor one, no single individual would be found responsible. In contrast to this Japanese model, decisions in American companies are usually made by top-level executives. Failure of a project or idea can be easily spotted and blame placed upon one individual, often causing executives to be at great risk of losing their jobs.

The impact of all these employment-related systems on conflict management in Japan is manifold. As a result of the stringent order, many potential conflicts of an employment nature are averted. Problems concerning parity between compensation for various employees, age differentials between superiors and subordinates, individual negotiations about raises and promotions, and intracompany nepotism are largely eliminated. Accordingly, many of the types of conflicts experienced in a Western employment setting are not found or are seldom experienced in the Japanese organizational environment.

The institutional structures of Japanese conflict management are summarized by the model presented in Figure 3.1. The small boxes in the large box represent employees, and the large box represents the organization's culture and the lifetime employment system. The vertical and horizontal order reflect the seniority system and the *dohki* groups, respectively. The unique characteristic of a Japanese organization is that

Figure 3.1
Model of Japanese Conflict Management

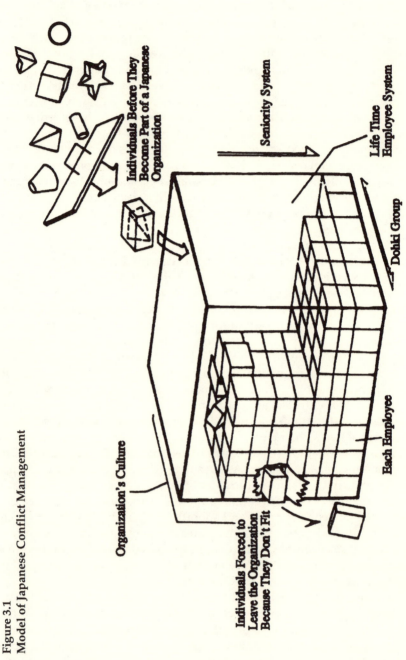

each member, who originally had different individual characteristics, is required to transform himself or herself into a uniform-shaped box in order to fit into the organization's structure and culture. Whoever fails to fit into this order might be pushed out from the organization's frame. What provides this rigid structure of the organization with some flexibility are the informal organizations and the Japanese unique decision-making system. Although the *intrapersonal* conflict of individuals is often relatively high under such organizational structures, the interpersonal conflicts are greatly minimized.

STYLES OF HANDLING INTERPERSONAL CONFLICT

Of the five styles (integrating, obliging, dominating, compromising, and avoiding), the Japanese prefer without question the avoiding style. In repeated samples of Japanese managers to the statement "organizations would be better off if conflict could be eliminated," Japanese agree very strongly. American managers disagree strongly.

Avoiding

On a behavioral level, there are a number of techniques commonly used by the Japanese to avoid conflict. Many of these techniques are not uncommon in cultures around the world, but they provide particular insight into the Japanese conflict management scheme. Some of the more prominent types of behavioral techniques used to manage conflict in Japan were outlined in detail by Krauss, Rohlen, and Steinhoff (1984, chap. 3). A brief description of how they are utilized follows.

One of the most effective techniques used is sometimes referred to as triadic management. To avoid confrontation between one another, the Japanese often create a triad with another outside individual to manage the situation. Conflict between the two parties may be communicated through the third party in an indirect manner. The third party, as an intermediary, represents both individuals. Sometimes the third party may take a more active role as an arbiter in situations where there is an apparent stalemate. In such a situation, the third party, who is respected by both other individuals, may provide a breakthrough by presenting her- or himself as the person on whose behalf the other two parties are to resolve the conflict. She or he urges the conflicting parties to relent so that she or he can "save face (*kao*)," with an implicit threat that she or he will take offense if their intervention is not heeded. In order to prevent humiliation to the arbiter, both parties may comply, even though they might prefer to remain at conflict with one another. Though this triadic management technique is by no means unique to Japan, it is utilized extensively, and provides one of the greatest vehicles for conflict management within the culture.

Compromising

A variant of triadic management, known as displacement, often can manifest itself in a variety of ways. Usually the displacement will take place in the form of an offended individual attempting to convey his or her anger or resentment to a third party, who is in a far more favorable position to transfer the feelings of the injured party to the injuring party in a manner that is less conflicting. As an example, a middle-aged contractor complains about his father-in-law, a retired contractor whose business he has inherited, for disagreeing with his modern way of living and doing business. The father-in-law will never tell his son-in-law directly of his disapproval, but will scold the employees about the shape and direction of the company. All parties including the employee understand that this is a criticism levied at the son-in-law. The son-in-law consoles his employees by reassuring them the remarks are not aimed at them.

Obliging

Another technique often utilized to avoid direct confrontation is commonly referred to as conflict acceptance. Instead of rejecting or correcting an undesirable state of affairs, the individual persuades her- or himself or is advised by someone else to accept the situation. This somewhat fatalistic or deterministic approach is rooted in the strong Buddhist influence on the culture throughout the history of Japan. Japanese tend to accept things *arugamama* (as they are) rather than to struggle to improve the situation. In general, when asked to do something difficult or unpleasant, such as working overtime or *tanshinfunin* (to take a position in another city, leaving one's family behind), the typical Japanese response would be to accept it rather than to complain or reject the request.

Integrating

Another less-utilized technique employed to avoid direct confrontation may be referred to as self-aggression or self-confrontation. In this technique, one party expresses a grievance against another by exaggerated compliance. An employee protests a transfer to another division within the company by declaring that he or she is indeed thankful for the transfer. If one is denigrated by another with a derogatory label such as "You are a failure," a likely response may be "Yes, I am truly a failure." What appears to be compliance on the surface is meant to be understood as remonstrative compliance, the purpose of which is to arouse guilt in the offending party. In its extreme expression, suicides have been committed surrounding recent disclosures of major scandals involving bribery, such as the cases of Lockheed, KDD, and others.

Dominating

This style of conflict resolution is contrary to the very nature of the Japanese character and consequently is not used.

ALTERNATIVE DISPUTE MANAGEMENT

The first experience most foreign businesspeople have with how conflict is managed in Japan is in the negotiation process. Table 3.1 identifies some of the key differences between the negotiation style of the Japanese and the Americans.

In the American style of negotiating, it is assumed that the details at hand are going to be ironed out at the negotiating table. All issues are open to public debate; arguing with the "opponent" is acceptable. Zimmerman (1985) notes that "American negotiating teams . . . tend to arrive in Japan armed with the conviction that it is time to lay down the law. They lecture and condescend to those they have come to meet as if they were converting savages to the one true faith" (p. 284). This style is in direct contrast to the Japanese style of conflict management and negotiation.

Consistent with the *ringi*-system, "Japanese perceive the negotiation almost as the ritualistic enactment of a predetermined agreement. They look with horror on the confrontation that the Americans expect at the table. Rather, the Japanese prefer to attempt persuasion behind the scenes, where neither side is in danger of losing face" (Moran, 1985, p. 76). At the negotiating table the Japanese are looking to finalize the details that have already been ironed out by their subordinates.

Moran further notes that "in negotiations, the Japanese strive for a 'meeting of hearts' and Japanese negotiators are not solely concerned with the 'bottom line' or end results" (p. 20). It is human relations that matter and saving another person's face is far more important than the actual business being negotiated.

The Western manager today must adopt a negotiating style that both suits the business objectives and still accommodate the Japanese cultural approach to negotiating. Zimmerman (1985) addresses the dual-objective approach: "The way to coax the Japanese into appreciating one's point of view, and the business concept that one is trying to sell to them, is to adopt a self-effacing and humble role while at the same time being quietly forceful whenever necessary or appropriate" (p. 97).

It is common in American circles to have a lawyer present during the negotiation process. The American negotiators prepare for battle and they use the lawyer as one of their effective weapons. This practice stems essentially from a lack of trust, and the presence of a lawyer is provided to put the other party at a psychological disadvantage. However, "during negotiations in Japan, the lawyer is rarely present, but the contract will be re-

Table 3.1
Negotiation Styles of Japanese and Americans

Japanese	Americans
Emotional sensitivity is highly valued	Emotional sensitivity is not highly valued
Indirect and unassertive	Direct and assertive
Soft sell and ambiguous	Hard sell and to the point
Not argumentative, quiet when right	Argumentative when right or wrong, but impersonal
Conciliatory	Confrontational
Favors nonverbal communication	Favors verbal communication
Group decision-making consensus	Teamwork provides input to a decision-maker
Face-saving crucial. Decision often made on basis of saving someone from embarrassment.	Decisions made on a cost benefit basis. Face-saving does not always matter.
Values humility	Values eloquence
Generally restricted, quiet style	Somewhat dramatic, animated style
Relatively formal style	Relatively informal style
Ample use of silence; pauses	Avoid silences
Avoids public disagreements	May disagree in public at negotiations
Table negotiating to learn about associates, gather data; to confirm and reveal what has been decided intra-organizationally	Expects public table decision-making
Cultivate a good emotional social setting for decision-making. Get to know decision-makers	Decision-making impersonal. Avoid involvements, conflict of interest

viewed by the legal department, and in important and complex situations the *ringi-sho* will be passed through the legal department for comment and approval" (Moran, 1985, p. 22). The Japanese are concerned with the legal implications of the contract or agreement reached, but having a lawyer present during negotiations breaks a cultural taboo by openly acknowledging mistrust of the other party.

Another critical dynamic in the negotiation process reflects the strong impact of the seniority system upon Japanese interactions. The negotiating person or persons on the team must be near the same age as their Japanese counterparts. "No matter how brilliant and dedicated a female or younger official is, such people simply have no credibility in Japan" (Zimmerman, 1985, p. 285). Even though Western women are treated with greater business respect than Japanese women, male chauvinism is extreme in negotiations and female negotiators often experience difficulties. Negotiators for Japanese companies tend to have twenty to twenty-five years of experience with their companies before being asked to speak for their companies. They will expect the same of their counterparts and have outright refused to deal with "youngsters" in the past. The Western negotiator must also have the consent to represent the company and to speak for it during specific negotiations. If the negotiator has to call the head office to clarify details or to get permission to accept a given proposal, the Japanese will refuse to take that person seriously.

DISCUSSION

When meeting a Japanese negotiator for the first time, it is a good idea to have a respected Japanese intermediary make the initial introductions. Although this may seem unnecessary, it ensures that the proper formalities are effectively dealt with and also presents the company in a good light, since the Japanese go-between is endorsing the company with his or her good reputation.

In contrast to the American negotiator, the Japanese negotiator makes very good use of silence as a negotiating tool. Silence causes American negotiators to feel uncomfortable because they don't know how to interpret this silence. As Moran (1985) explains, silence can mean one of several things to the Japanese: "respect for the person who has spoken, consideration of an important point, or disagreement with what has been said" (p. 90). One should not immediately assume that something has gone wrong, but should use this time to look back over what has been discussed and to plan for what is coming up next in the negotiations. Rather than responding instantly to Japanese points made during a discussion, Americans should use silence as a tool to keep the Japanese on their feet. Silence provides the opportunity for American negotiators to carefully contemplate their next move.

Negotiations take a great deal of time in Japan, and American negotiators must plan for lengthy negotiations. The Japanese want to take their time to learn about their counterparts and to evaluate whether they can expect to have a successful relationship with them in the future. Rushing negotiations and faking a friendship will only leave the Western negotiators in the room alone.

The Japanese negotiation process is based on the importance of maintaining harmony in relationships. Norms are established concerning obligations to others, benevolence, and the importance of others' attitudes. Application of this ideal precludes open conflict. An inferior is expected to defer to a superior. The ideal way to resolve conflict is through harmonious cooperation coupled with the "warrior ethic" of assertiveness and persistence in negotiations.

If negotiation is based on harmony, a formal setting with each party advocating its own position becomes undesirable. Unplanned compromise, submission to threats, admission of inconsistencies, and other such possibilities make it a face-threatening event. Instead, the Japanese see negotiation as a fluid irrational process, calling for diligent preparation. Instead of addressing issues directly and openly stating positions and counterproposals, they prefer to infer the other parties' assessment of the situation.

The Japanese often repeat previously stated positions, using highly ambiguous language and appearing to be inconsistent. The goal of this process is a just, fair, and proper deal and, more generally, a long-term harmonious relationship with their counterparts and their corporations.

A detailed analysis of audiotaped or videotaped Japanese/American *actual* negotiations may be necessary to test the theory presented in this chapter, and in other books on Japanese management style. The theories then can be tested and modified as necessary. Observing and documenting actual negotiations will be the challenge of successful researchers.

"Conflict," like the word "culture," has no single agreed-upon definition. Thomas (1992) defined it as the process that starts when one party feels that the other has frustrated, or is about to frustrate, some of their concerns. Another definition of conflict is what results when two or more persons attempt to occupy the same space at the same time. Regardless of which definition we accept, the management of conflict is a major issue at the personal and organizational levels. Ineffectively managed conflict decreases the effectiveness of the individuals involved and the ability of the organization to achieve its objectives.

Most managers are now viewing conflict as a healthy, natural and inevitable part of relationships and organizations. The belief that conflict can be constructive requires that problems be addressed directly and that people can be motivated to search for solutions to these problems. This chapter demonstrated that Japan in its conflict resolution modes does not agree.

APPENDIX: GLOSSARY OF IMPORTANT TERMS

dohki   peer group that consists of all the employees who began their careers with the company during a given year

kao   face; pride, self-esteem, and reputation; personal honor

nemawashi	preparing the groundwork; root binding
ningensei	state of being human; calls for the stressing of relationship communication over task communication; values smooth, gracious public relations over all else
ringi	a system in which co-workers circulate a proposal in document form (*ringi-sho*) around the company; on this document large numbers of people affix their seals as a sign that they have seen the proposal and will not actively oppose what it says
uchi	in; in-group; member of group
soto	out; out-group; not one of the group
wa	harmony; involves cooperation, trust, sharing, and warmth; the element that holds the Japanese society together

REFERENCES

Benedict, R. (1954). *The chrysanthemum and the sword*. Tokyo: Charles E. Tuttle.

Cosier, R. A., Schwenk, C. R., & Dalton, D. R. (1992). Managerial decision making in Japan, the U.S., and Hong Kong. *International Journal of Conflict Management, 3*, 151–160.

Hofstede, G. (1980). *Culture's consequences: International differences in work-related values*. Beverly Hills, CA: Sage.

Hofstede, G. (1991). *Cultures and organizations: Software of the mind*. London: McGraw-Hill.

Krauss, E. S., Rohlen, T. P., & Steinhoff, P. G. (Eds.). (1984). *Conflict in Japan*. Honolulu: University of Hawaii Press.

Likert, R., & Likert, J. G. (1976). *New ways of managing conflict*. New York: McGraw-Hill.

Moran, R. T. (1985). *Getting your yen's worth: How to negotiate with Japan, Inc.* Houston: Gulf.

Thomas, K. W. (1992). Conflict and negotiation processes in organizations. In M. D. Dunnette & L. M. Hough (Eds.), *Handbook of industrial & organizational psychology*, Vol. 3 (2nd ed., pp. 651–717). Palo Alto, CA: Consulting Psychologists Press.

Ting-Toomey, S., Gao, G., Trubisky, P., Yang, Z., Kim, H. S., Lin, S. -L., & Nishida, T. (1991). Culture, face maintenance, and styles of handling interpersonal conflict: A study in five cultures. *International Journal of Conflict Management, 2*, 275–296.

Zimmerman, M. (1985). *How to do business with the Japanese*. New York: Random House.

4

THE NETHERLANDS

Ben Emans, Peter Laskewitz, and Evert van de Vliert

In any discussion on conflict handling in Dutch organizations, inevitably, sooner or later, some peculiar terms characterizing Dutch society are used: *consensus society* (*consensusmaatschappij*), *conference society* or *talk society* (*vergadermaatschappij*), and *consultation society* (*overlegmaatschappij*). According to these characterizations, Dutch people plainly do not follow quick and easy procedures to reach agreements. Conflicts are not easily settled by mechanisms like majority rules, formal discretionary power, moral authority, or aggression and force. Instead, when conflicts threaten to come up, Dutch people resort to quite a repertory of well-regulated types of deliberations.

In organizations, this feature of Dutch social life, which is apparent to both Dutch and foreign observers (Van der Velden, 1990; Willems & Cottaar, 1989; Zahn, 1984), is reflected in long and often boring discussions by self-conceited quarreling managers, who make extensive use of references to all kinds of rules and moral principles. The main characteristics of these discussants are a formal, stiff, and cold approach of each other, along with a high degree of tolerance toward each other, together with a dislike of polarization, and a deep-rooted sense of justice. Rules and reasoning seem to be the only tools Dutch managers are inclined to apply in conflicts.

This portrait of Dutch organizational life will be elaborated in the sections to follow. First, the sociohistorical background of Dutch society will be sketched, which will help the reader to understand the main lines in the picture. Second, some empirical evidence will be presented that gives concrete form to them. Finally, to complete the picture, a number of typical Dutch dispute management procedures will be described.

SOCIAL, CULTURAL, AND ECONOMIC FACTORS

The Netherlands (Nederland, Low Countries) is a small country in Western Europe, where a distinctive language is spoken (Dutch), and which is densely populated by more than 15 million people. It was initially founded in 1579 and actually came into being in 1648, when the last remnants of the Spanish yoke were shaken off, with the Spanish Hapsburg dynasty, who ruled the country until then, being defeated by local revolutionaries. This Dutch Revolution chiefly had economic origins, as the prosperous Dutch merchant world had suffered from exploitation and restrictions carried out by the centralized political Hapsburg system.

What resulted was quite a new phenomenon. It was called a republique, or even *the* Republique, being unique for its constitutional features. In fact, the Republique of the United Netherlands was no more than a loose coalition of seven provinces (one of which, the richest one, was called Holland; its name is often used, unjustifiably, to refer to the whole of the Netherlands). Each province had its own identity and each constituted a ministate itself. What connected them was a shared need for freedom. This interdependence did not allow a powerful political center to arise.

The resulting social segmentation was further fostered by a strong religious factor. A denominational-geographical division had originated accidentally in 1609 when hostilities between Spanish and revolutionary armies were temporarily suspended. Regions that happened to be occupied by the Spanish at that time became Catholic and by and large have remained so until today. The other regions became Protestant areas. Unlike other European nations, the country thus found itself situated simultaneously at both sides of the Rome-Reformation demarcation line.

Social segmentation as such has never disappeared from the Dutch scene. Indeed, when the nation came of age a number of new distinctions, especially of a confessional and ideological nature, were added, and old distinctions, like the geographical ones, lost something of their salience. Basically, the cultural format has remained the same and still encompasses a population of people belonging to quite distinctive social groups (Boissevain & Verrips, 1989). From the very beginning this constituted a challenge for the nation-to-be.

This sociocultural condition allowed a typical Dutch phenomenon, which started some 150 years ago, to arise gradually. It is a conflict-prevention and regulation mechanism, which amounts to the inverse of "LAT (living-apart-together) relationships"—namely: living together apart. The sociological technical term for the latter is *pillarization (verzuiling;* see Daalder, 1966; Steininger, 1977; Van Schendelen, 1984a; Kriesi, 1990), which portrays a society composed of a number of separate pillars, standing side by side. A very essential characteristic of this society is the absence of between-pillar status differentiation, or power differentiation. By no means does the pillarized society bear any likeness to the stratified caste system, or to the apartheid system with its built-in inequalities (it is noteworthy, nonetheless, that the apartheid system was a product of white South Africans of Dutch origin; *apartheid* is a Dutch word).

A second essential characteristic of pillarization is the low level of between-pillar communication. Communication is virtually restricted to the top level of the society. At the common national "roof," supported by the pillars together, the elites meet to settle their differences. The society became "closed at the bottom, and open at the top" (Goudsblom, 1968, p. 124).

Pillarization culminated in the first half of this century. In those days there were Roman Catholic, Protestant, and Socialist pillars, the latter existing quite apart from a much smaller Communist one (Van Schendelen, 1984b; Van Mierlo, 1986). The first two, the confessional pillars, were socioeconomically mixed. The third, the "Red Family," consisting mainly of the lower strata of the population, was socioeconomically more homogeneous and had a nonconfessional orientation. Sometimes a fourth main pillar is distinguished: a conservative-liberal one, nonconfessional in its orientation, and consisting mainly of relatively higher strata of the population. As can be seen, pillarization was based on both religious and class distinctions.

Each of the pillars tended to have its own norms, values, habits, beliefs, symbols, celebrations, and so on, as well as its own political party, broadcasting system, schools, newspapers and periodicals, associations for scouts or other juvenile work, sporting clubs, and labor union. Companies, too, large and small ones alike, were often associated with just one pillar. In short, the pillars constituted complete tribelike societies.

The social reality of most Dutch citizens thus became bifold. On the one hand, they lived in their own social group (their own pillar), and derived a considerable part of their social identity from that group. On the other hand, they were faced with the undeniable existence, near at hand, of other groups, which consisted of strangers who were just as respectable as their own people. A sociological condition of equivalent, yet distinct, autonomous parties thus emerged as one of the essential attributes of Dutch society. At the social-psychological level this was reflected in the cultural axiom of antidogmatism in public life, or, as it is called, "tolerant acceptance of people of different persuasions" (*andersdenkenden*, a very common Dutch word). This tolerance axiom fitted in perfectly with the merchant origin of the nation. As merchants all over the world, the Dutch were pragmatically tolerant toward other cultures and religions, because this smoothed the way for doing business. In fact, the first drafts of the constitution of the Republique (1579) already stated that "no one may be prosecuted or investigated in the cause of religion" (Goudsblom, 1968, p. 18). Sociohistorically it is therefore no surprise to see that the Netherlands scored high with regard to cultural and religious tolerance in a study of national cultures in Europe (Stoetzel, 1983, pp. 286–287).

The pillarization system reduced the probability of between-pillar conflicts. When such conflicts did occur, one could, of course, take them to court. Apart from that, no other supersystem was available for settling disagreements. There was no norm of one subculture dominating another, nor could overarching nationalistic feelings undo intersubcultural contrasts. The only conflict-handling procedure that was compatible with the tolerance axiom was the acceptance of disagreements and the habit to talk them over in a search for compromise and consensus. Hence, a strong tradition of consensus-directed discussion procedures could develop. Lijphart (1968) showed how at the society's highest level (the "roof"), this tradition developed into a refined art of conflict management, with a number of rules of the game to depoliticize issues. In Lijphart's view, it is this elite behavior, together with strong within-pillar social control, that explains the stability of the plural (labeled *consociational*) Dutch society (for critics and review, see Van Schendelen, 1984b; Scholten, 1980).

Metaphorically, Dutch people are said to often play the double role of merchant and clergy. In many other cultures this would amount to sheer incompatibility. Under Dutch circumstances it is almost mandatory. The merchant component of the role reflects the origin of the Dutch nation, making Dutch people and pillars both selfish and tolerant/respectful toward others. The clergy component serves to reconcile these two traits. It provides the rules of the game for the delicate consensus that has to be constructed permanently, such as repertories of moral and other principles to be referred to, vocabularies of ideological terms to be used, and complicated lines of reasoning.

Starting two or three decades ago a number of developments set in, notably proliferation of cultural diversity, deconfessionalization, and emancipation (Wierdsma & Bomers, 1982; Thung, Peelen & Kingmans, 1982), that contributed to the so-called depillarization (*ontzuiling*)—that is, the collapse of the pillar system (Van Mierlo, 1986). Pillarization, however, has left its marks. The above-mentioned tradition of between-pillar dispute resolution by talking became even more relevant than ever before as within-pillar specific traditions faded away one by one. In the next section we will see how this cultural fact is mirrored in organizational life.

MANAGERIAL STYLES

A nice picture of a Dutch organization can be found in Schein's (1985) book on organizational culture and leadership. In that book two examples of organizational cultures are described in a detailed way, one pertaining to a Dutch multinational, pseudonymously called Multi. Striking features of Multi's culture are the force of formal and informal rules, the reliance on old and wise organization members, the power of experts, a strong status-consciousness, punctuality in planning and control activities, and a high value attached to protocol. The function of all of these cultural elements is to prevent a polarization of conflicts. "Meetings and conferences have to be well defined, have a clear purpose accepted by all, and be planned with rank and appropriate deference in mind" (Schein, 1986, p. 106). Weber's bureaucratic ideals of rationality and formalization can easily be recognized.

What Schein describes is valuable as a concretization of what has been said about the Dutch people's preference for, and dependence on, rules and reasoning in conflict handling. It shows how conflicts in a Dutch organization tend to be depersonalized and depolarized by means of a strong system of rituals and norms. Thanks to such a system, the Dutch manager can take forceful action to defend his own interests, without being accused of attacking others, and without endangering feelings of harmony and consensus. The only price to be paid for this outcome is time: the rituals are very time-consuming.

Some quantitative intercultural comparison studies, bearing upon the theme of conflict handling in organizations, fit in nicely with the statements above. Rosenstein (1985) collected a number of cooperativeness indexes of managers in the Netherlands and eleven other countries. One of them consisted of the time it took before agreement was reached in negotiations. As to this index the Dutch subsample turned out to be the unquestioned leader, with more than twice the amount of time-consumption as compared to the U.S. sample, and surpassing countries like India, France, the United Kingdom, and Germany. Quite comparable results were found in a study by Heller, Drenth, Koopman, and Rus (1988, p. 128): in Dutch organizations, compared to English and Yugoslavian organizations, deliberations appeared to take larger amounts of time.

According to Rosenstein, his results indicate a lack of cooperativeness in the Dutch management culture. In his view, time consumption is seen as a consequence of resistance to agreement, and as sheer postponement of agreement. To insiders of the Dutch culture, this interpretation sounds absurd. From a Dutch point of view, a quickly reached agreement probably conceals unsolved disagreements. It is suspect, it has the flavor of unfinished rituals, and it gives evidence of a disregard for oneself, or a disregard for the other people, or both. A short negotiation time, rather than a long one, would be an indication of noncooperativeness in Dutch settings.

Accordingly, when other cooperative indexes, used in Rosenstein's study, are taken into account, the comparison between the Netherlands and other countries yields quite other results. At the far extreme, on an index of self-reported cooperativeness, the Dutch sample was the champion in the sense of being the most cooperative. Clearly, the Rosenstein results portray the Dutch manager as someone who concerns him- or herself with the plight of other parties, without confusing the other parties' interests with his or her own well-guarded interests.

That Dutch manager is thus driven both by self-interest and a need for harmony. This does not emerge only from observations like those mentioned above. In a more fundamental way it is supported by studies of organizational culture as well. Hofstede (1980) analyzed extensive files of information, collected in 1967 and 1973, on organizational cultures of IBM plants in different countries, including the Netherlands. His data revealed four dimensions of national culture. The first one, called power distance, represents the amount of power difference between hierarchical levels, which is found most acceptable by organization members. The second one, uncertainty avoidance, represents attributes like the need for security, the dependence upon experts, and rule-orientedness. The third one, individualism (versus collectivism) represents adherence to private opinions, concern for one's own interests, and universalism instead of particularism with regard to rights and obligations. The fourth dimension is femininity (versus masculinity) and represents the willingness to serve others, strive for harmony, and sympathize with the weak.

According to Hofstede's study, the Dutch organizational culture turned out to be characterized by moderately small power distance, moderately weak uncertainty avoidance, high individualism, and high femininity. The last two elements are especially noteworthy; together they form a rather exceptional combination. Of all forty countries studied, only the Scandinavian countries shared this feature with the Netherlands.

The more or less counterintuitive distinction Hofstede made between masculinism-femininism on the one hand, and collectivism-individualism on the other hand, thus appeared to be indispensable for an adequate description of Dutch and Scandinavian organizational cultures. The individualism/feminism combination that emerged in the research results reflects the linking of self-interest and tolerance of others in the Dutch culture and, more fundamentally, the above-mentioned postpillarization conditions of modern Dutch public life.

Confirming the feminine tendency of Dutch people, research in progress by one of the authors showed that Dutch managers have more sympathy for relatively weak conflict parties than managers from other countries in Western Europe have. In a questionnaire study, Dutch, German, Swiss, and French general managers in the graphics industry were confronted with the same scenario. Two subordinates in conflict were depicted, one having much less power than the other. The Dutch managers supported the weaker party as much as the stronger party, while the German, Swiss, and French managers clearly supported the stronger party only.

About ten years after Hofstede's research, Trompenaars (n.d.) performed a comparable study that provides additional evidence for the picture of Dutch conflict management that is taking shape here. He compared ten firms in different countries with regard to their organizational culture. Five were plants of Royal-Dutch/Shell, with one located in the Netherlands. Another five were independent enterprises active in the hosiery business, with one located in the Netherlands.

Contrary to Hofstede, Trompenaars used a one-dimensional model of organizational culture as a starting point of his research. Metaphorically he labeled it "right brain versus left brain conception of organization." One pole, left brain, stands for things like universalism, formalism, impersonality, and rationality in relationships between organization members. The other pole, right brain, stands for the opposite: affectivity, collectivism, and so on. Clearly, Trompenaars contrasted masculinity/individualism on the one hand, and femininity/collectivism on the other, thus confounding Hofstede's two relatively independent dimensions.

Knowing Hofstede's results, we might expect the one-dimensional model to break down in the Dutch case, and so it turned out to do. Specifically, the two Dutch companies in the sample got a high "left brain" rating (surpassed only by a U.S. company), on an item that straightforwardly reflected individualism (the organization seen as a functional system versus a group of people), whereas, in contrast, they got a high "right brain" rating on an item that reflected femininity (referring to affectivity and mutual compassion of organization members). Typically, the Dutch enterprises were close to both poles. In his conclusions, Trompenaars disregards these and similar details in his results, but undeniably they force the one-dimensional model to be refined in order to do justice to Dutch reality. To be more concrete: although unnoticed, Trompenaar's findings once again provide support for the Dutch organization to be pictured as having members with equal high concern for one's own and for other's goals.

STYLES OF HANDLING INTERPERSONAL CONFLICT

In the five-styles model of conflict handling (integrating, obliging, dominating, avoiding, and compromising), a distinction may be made between styles of equal concern for self and others (integrating, avoiding, compromising), and styles of unequal concern for self and others (obliging, dominating). Given the Dutch need for harmony and consensus (femininity) as described in the preceding section, one might expect the equal-concern styles to be preferred in Dutch organizations, as compared to organizations in more masculine cultures. Comparative research is very scarce with regard to this question, but as far as findings are available, they confirm these expectations.

In a self-report study by Leung et al. (1990), Canadian and Dutch subjects were asked to estimate their behavior intentions in hypothetical conflict situations. The Canada-Netherlands comparison is interesting, because in the aforementioned study by Hofstede, both countries scored high in individualism, whereas they differed as to their degree of femininity/masculinity, Canada being about neutral on this dimension, and the Netherlands being rather feminine.

Leung et al.'s results are perfectly intelligible when this femininity/masculinity difference is taken into account. Reformulated in terms of the five-styles model, their results show that the Dutch subjects, compared to the Canadian subjects, had stronger preferences for the equal-concern styles avoiding and compromising/integrating, and weaker preferences for the unequal-concern styles dominating and obliging.

In one other study similar comparisons were made (Heller et al., 1988, p. 141), this time between some Dutch companies on the one hand, and some English and Yugoslavian companies on the other hand. Unfortunately, only a one-dimensional model was used to measure the conflict modes, but some transpositions to the five-styles model are possible. The one dimension, called *open facing versus forcing,* equals the integrating-dominating continuum. On that continuum the Dutch companies scored considerably higher (more integrating) than the other companies. Simultaneously, they scored lowest as to the frequency of conflicts, which implies a tendency to evade conflicts. Taken together, this again shows that members in Dutch organizations feel most comfortable when they stick close to the equal-concern styles: integrating, avoiding, and compromising. We now turn to the question of what shape these, and the other two styles, take in the reality of Dutch organizations.

Integrating

Concrete attempts to integrate, such as all conflict-handling behavior in Dutch situations, are characterized primarily by ritualization and formalization. Parties have at their disposal many sets of gamelike rules, whose function is to depersonalize the arguments so that somehow the personal harmony between discussants is maintained, even when they harass each other with sharp attacks.

Outsiders are sometimes struck by the stiffness, bluntness, and insensitivity Dutch people display toward each other in formal conferences, and are the more surprised when after such a conference the same people appear to behave like friends. This paradox is explained by the fact that impersonality and formality are part of the game. The game character of the situation allows all parties involved in an issue to express their private views, and simultaneously prevents the resulting clashes to become harmful. Part of the game is also that all participants amply take and get time to expose their stand. Concern for self and concern for other parties are thus reconciled in this time-consuming but, for the participants, satisfying way.

Obliging, Dominating

It is very difficult to sketch pictures of the practices of obliging and dominating in Dutch organizations. One is inclined to attribute this difficulty to the fact that both obliging and dominating are somehow not done in Dutch organizations: as said above, there is a preference for equal-concern conflict-handling styles. It goes too far, however, to state that the two unequal-concern styles, obliging and dominating, are practically absent.

The truth is that obliging and dominating, both being culturally suspect, are mainly practiced in an indirect and implicit way, and consequently remain almost invisible. Undoubtedly, a lot of shown-off compromising or integrating is in fact a combination of obliging and dominating in disguise. For instance, conflict-outcomes may be presented as the result of the application of some long-standing, agreed-upon rule, while in fact it is the result of a backstage power game. That presentation is needed to save the face of winners and losers, of dominators and obligers, alike.

Avoiding, Compromising

Despite the availability of conflict-handling rules and rites, and despite the long time one is always willing to spend on resolving conflicts, good and satisfying resolutions may be held off. Many conflict issues just do not allow a resolution that will satisfy all parties involved. In such cases Dutch people seem to have no other choice but to continue the discussions, patiently postponing decisions. The postponement may result in different outcomes. Sometimes it leads to a chronic state of nonresolution, sometimes to a kind of quasi-resolution, with far-from-unequivocally worded agreements, and sometimes to detailed, real compromises. Often, however, the outcome is a complicated mixture of those forms of conflict avoiding and compromising. In this opaque way, and often difficult to distinguish from each other, avoiding and compromising form part of the practice of Dutch conflict handling.

With respect to conflict prevention and conflict solution, a number of legal and semilegal constructions have been developed where the styles, described here, are applied in a special way. In the next section these will be briefly described.

ALTERNATIVE DISPUTE MANAGEMENT

In Dutch organizational life participation rites abound. They are characterized by extensive rules and delineated rights and obligations of parties in whatever context. An example is the legally prescribed participation council (*medezeggenschapsraad*), where, according to very precise legislation, employees may try to influence the company strategy. Comparable constructions exist in schools in order to regulate participation by parents, pupils, and personnel, and in universities, where students and faculties are supposed to invest time and energy in participation at all levels of decision-making. The function of these bodies is to smooth the antagonisms that exist within organizations.

There are more elements within Dutch organization structures that have this function. Another typical one is a particular system of direct participative decision-making on the shop floor, called work consultation (*werkoverleg*). It is a system of quite regular (often once a week) and formal consultation between a supervisor and his or her subordinates as a group, aimed at participation in and influence on the decision-making process with regard to the common work situation.

These and similar constructions are highly relevant for the conflict regulation in organizations. They clearly fulfill the need to involve all parties, irrespective of their positions, in the settlement of whatever disagreements there are. Although they are not commonly viewed as conflict-regulating tools, they undeniably have a function in the early phases of conflicts and help to prevent polarization and escalation.

Among organizations (such as in union-management relations) at the between-organization level, and in the public domain, similar constructions exist. The most notorious example is the Social Economic Council (Sociaal Economische Raad, or SER), where representatives of employers and employees, together with some independent wise and respected individuals, meet to formulate advice with regard to socioeconomic policies for the central government. It is a conflict-prevention tool at the highest political level. The Dutch/American economist A. Klamer (1990), after having studied the SER history, concluded that politics in the Netherlands seems to be embedded in a culture of discussions, making use of rhetoric inaccessible to foreigners. His terse characterization applies to all spheres of Dutch public life: "To evade class-struggle, Dutch people prefer to sit together around a table."

In addition to these conflict-prevention tools, certain conflict-resolution traditions have been developed. They may be called mediation rituals and can be found in all spheres of public life. The common format is the appointment, by the conflicting parties themselves, of a group of mediators who are supposed to be wise and independent. For that to be true, the group ideally incorporates in itself the different backgrounds of all parties involved. On the societal level the old pillars can often be recognized in the composition of such groups. This is most clearly the case with the State Council (*Raad van State*), the highest institution of the state, which has the major task of advising on controversial law concepts and settling disagreements between governmental and other parties.

Another example is the common appointment of ad hoc "colleges of wise men" (as they are sometimes called), to mediate in prolonged labor-management conflicts. There is no substantial tradition of strikes in the Netherlands. In the period between 1983 and 1988, for instance, only 13 working days were lost yearly per 1,000 employees (United States: 94, West Germany: 45, France: 54, United Kingdom: 362, but Japan: 7) (Uitterhoeve, 1990, p. 164). Similar data on the 1972 to 1981 period are given by Walsh (1983, pp. 157–164), and on the 1956 to 1965 period by Windmuller (1969, p. 396). Associations of employers and labor unions do not like to use force or resort to arbitration by court. Instead they prefer to talk with each other, if necessary with the assistance of a mediator. More generally speaking one might say that the Dutch culture is mediation-prone, rather than arbitration-prone. In the study by Leung et al. (1990) this is clearly marked in the difference between a Dutch sample of students and an equivalent Canadian sample.

The prevalence of the ombudsman phenomenon in many spheres of public life provides another type of mediation tradition. The ombudsman is a person whose function is dedicated completely to mediation in special kinds of conflicts. There is a large ombudsman institute, for instance, whose responsibility is to handle complaints of individual citizens about activities of the national or local administration. Another example is the ombudswoman in companies whose task is to help female employees in conflicts with management, notably including sexual harassment. A crucial feature of ombudsmen or ombudswomen is their independence, which makes them trustworthy for all parties involved. In no sense do they have any formal power. Just as in the case of the colleges of wise men, the basic ombuds-formula is the neutralizing of conflicts by means of agreed-upon procedures.

DISCUSSION

Dutch conflict management, as it is sketched in this chapter, can be considered to be the product of a dialectical relationship between a sociogenetical and a psychogenetical process. Sociogenesis and psychogenesis are terms coined by the sociologist N. Elias (1976) to denote two processes that together constitute the process of civilization (*Prozess der Zivilisation*). Sociogenesis is the process of changing material conditions in a society, whereas psychogenesis is the process of changing norms, values, rites, and concepts that are taken for granted in that society. In Elias' view the two processes impinge upon each other, and can only be understood in relation to each other.

In the case of conflict handling in Dutch organizations, the sociogenetical process includes the pillarization process—that is, the process of social segmentation, which results in the living together apart of distinct subpopulations. Another element consists of the development of conflict-management procedures, which contribute to a social reality of impersonal, procedural justice. In the society that results, ideally a party in a conflict seldom can say that it, or another party, has been overruled.

The corresponding psychogenetical process includes, at the level of attitudes, the development of what we called the cultural axiom of "tolerant acceptance of people of different persuasion." At the behavioral level, psychogenesis is primarily characterized by the development of the habit of conflict-management-by-talking, and of the preference for conflict styles on the equal-concern diagonal in the five-styles model: integrating, avoiding, and compromising. These elements, in spite of the widely divergent concrete forms they may assume, always constituted and still constitute, under different historical circumstances and in different societal contexts, the basic format of Dutch conflict handling.

The empirical evidence of these statements is scattered: a couple of empirical studies, historical data, information about existing procedures, and the everyday knowledge of the authors. However, without exception these sources of information tend to converge neatly, making it rather unimaginable that another picture could have been drawn. Many details, however, are open to further empirical investigation.

To corroborate the sociogenetical assumptions—for instance, systematic comparisons between Dutch conflict management habits and those in sociogenetically similar societies—would be useful. Another question pertains to intracultural differences. Undoubtedly the old and new pillars of Dutch society have their own conflict management cultures, but how these cultures look, how they are related to congenial cultures of other societies, and how they incorporate the above-sketched basic format of Dutch conflict management are still far from clear. These and other questions are generated by the socio/psychogenetical approach that underlay the preceding discussion. On the one hand this approach was indispensable in order to construct a more or less consistent picture of Dutch conflict handling, on the other hand it may provide indications for the direction of future research in that field.

ACKNOWLEDGEMENTS

Helpful comments on an earlier version of the text were given by Jan Pieter van Oudenhoven and Dean Tjosvold.

REFERENCES

Boissevain, J., & Verrips, J. (Eds.) (1989). *Dutch dilemmas: Anthropologists look at the Netherlands*. Assen: Van Gorcum.

Daalder, H. (1966). The Netherlands: Opposition in a segmented society. In R. A. Dahl (Ed.), *Political oppositions in Western democracies* (pp. 188–236). New Haven, CT: Yale University Press.

Elias, N. (1976). *Über den prozess de zivilisation* [On the process of civilisation]. Frankfurt am Main: Suhrkamp.

Goudsblom, J. (1968). *Dutch society.* New York: Random House.

Heller, F., Drenth, P., Koopman, P., & Rus, V. (1988). *Decisions in organizations: A three country study.* London: Sage.

Hofstede, G. (1980). *Culture's consequences: International differences in work-related values.* Beverly Hills, CA: Sage.

Klamer, A. (1990). *Verzuilde dromen: Veertig jaar SER* [Pillarized dreams: Forty years Social Economic Council]. Amsterdam: Balans.

Kriesi, H. (1990). Federalism and pillarization. *Acta Politica, 4,* 433–450.

Leung, K., Bond, M. H., Carment, D. W., Krishnan, L., & Liebrand, W.B.G. (1990). Effects of cultural femininity on preference methods of conflict processing: A cross-cultural study. *Journal of Experimental Social Psychology, 26,* 373–388.

Lijphart, A. (1968). *The politics of accommodation.* Berkeley: University of California Press.

Rosenstein, E. (1985). Cooperativeness and advancement of managers: An international perspective. *Human Relations, 38,* 1–21.

Schein, E. H. (1985). *Organizational culture and leadership.* San Francisco: Jossey-Bass.

Scholten, I. (1980). Does consociationalism exist? A critique of the Dutch experience. In R. Rose (Ed.), *Electoral participation: A comparative analysis* (pp. 329–354). Beverly Hills, CA: Sage.

Steininger, R. (1977). Pillarization and political parties. *Sociologische Gids, 24,* 242–257.

Stoetzel, J., (1983). *Les valeurs du temps présent: Une enquête Européenne* [Values nowadays: A European survey]. Paris: Presses Universitaires de France.

Thung, M. A., Peelen, G. J., & Kingmans, M. C. (1982). Dutch pillarisation on the move? Political destabilisation and religious change. *West European Politics, 5* (2), 127–148.

Trompenaars, F. (n.d.). *The organization of meaning and the meaning of organization: A comparative study of the conceptions of organizational structure in different cultures.* Doctoral dissertation, Wharton School, University of Pennsylvania.

Uitterhoeve, W. (Ed.). (1990). *De staat van Nederland* [The State of the Netherlands]. Nijmegen: SUN.

Van der Velden, B. (1990, October 25). Onze tegenspraakcultuur verbaast het buitenland [Our culture-of-controversies amazes foreigners]. *NRC-Handelsblad.*

Van Mierlo, H.J.G.A. (1986). Depillarisation and the decline of consociationalism in the Netherlands: 1970–85. *West European Politics, 9* (1), 97–119.

Van Schendelen, M.C.P.M. (Ed.). (1984a). Consociationalism, pillarization and conflictmanagement in the low countries [Special issue]. *Acta Politica, 19* (1).

———. (1984b). The views of Arend Lijphart and collected criticisms. *Acta Politica 19,* 19–55.

Walsh, K. (1983). *Strikes in Europe and the United States.* London: Frances Pinter Publishers.

Wierdsma, A.F.M., & Bomers, G.B.J. (1982). Conflict management in Dutch industrial relations: An analysis of recent developments, trends, and issues. In G.B.J. Bomers & R. B. Peterson (Eds.), *Conflict management and industrial relations* (pp. 303–325). Boston: Kluwer/Nijhoff.

Willems, W., & Cottaar, A. (1989). *Het beeld van Nederland: hoe zien Molukkers. Chinezen, woonwagenbewoners en Turken de Nederlanders en zichzelf?* [The image of the Netherlands: What do Moluccans, Chinese, caravan-dwellers and Turks think of Dutchmen and of themselves?] Amsterdam: Ambo.

Windmuller, J. P. (1969). *Labor relations in the Netherlands.* Ithaca, NY: Cornell University Press.

Zahn, E. (1984). *Das unbekannte Holland: Regenten. Rebellen und Reformatoren* [Unknown Holland: Regents, Rebels and Reformers]. Berlin: Siedler. Translated into Dutch (1989): *Regenten, rebellen en Reformatoren, een visie op Nederland en de Nederlanders.* Amsterdam: Uitgeverij Contact.

5

NORWAY

Jørn Kjell Rognes

In this chapter we explore the nature of conflict-management and negotiation behavior in Norway. The purpose is to examine how institutional and cultural factors affect the use of different conflict-management procedures and managerial behavior in negotiation processes. This chapter presents an explorative discussion of comparative conflict-management analysis with a focus on Norway. In doing so we draw upon anthropological literature on Norway, institutional sociology, and on my own work as a researcher and consultant in conflict management. Given the explorative nature of this analysis, conclusions are presented as testable propositions and not as confirmed results.

It is now widely accepted that a moderate amount of conflict is both necessary and unavoidable in organized systems (Rahim, 1992). The effect of conflict on individuals and organizations depends on how the conflicts are managed (Brett & Rognes, 1986). Conflict researchers have identified a variety of conflict-management procedures and behavioral styles used in conflict situations, and they have also made normative recommendations for how to handle conflict most constructively (Fisher & Ury, 1981; Tjosvold, 1989). But the conflict-management literature is predominantly American, and we have little knowledge about how actual and preferred ways of handling conflicts vary across nations. There is little knowledge about the applicability of American theories in other national contexts. This is unfortunate for two major reasons. First, conflict and conflict management are sensitive issues in most nations, and we need relevant theoretical frameworks for understanding the role of conflict in different cultures. Second, since multinational companies have subsidiaries in many countries, and since international negotiations are gaining importance for business organizations, cross-cultural conflict management will be a critical activity in many organizations.

The discussion in this chapter is limited to task-related conflicts in the organizational setting. We focus primarily on managerial behavior in informal conflict situations. Furthermore, when we discuss national characteristics in conflict behavior, we need an external reference point. In this chapter the United States is used for this purpose, because most conflict-handling literature has been developed within the American cultural context, and also because this author has experience from conflict research in American organizations.

SOCIAL, CULTURAL, AND ECONOMIC FACTORS

In discussing differences among nations, we distinguish between institutional and cultural causes of conflict-management. *Institutional factors* include the economic, political, social, legal, and demographic context of organizations. *Cultural factors* include the degree and form of homogeneity in the collective national mental programming. Institutional and cultural factors are, of course, interrelated and derived from a larger historical contextual reality. It is useful to distinguish the institutional setting from the cultural attributes of a nation for two reasons: (1) countries with fairly similar institutional systems may vary in terms of culture and vice versa; (2) institutional and cultural factors affect conflict management primarily at two different levels. Institutional factors will to a large extent influence the use of a specific conflict-management procedure when a potential conflict exists. They do so by providing the structural setup for conflict management. Cultural factors may primarily influence conflict management through the behavioral strategies used in the conflict-management process. They do so by influencing the behavioral inclinations of individuals.

Norway has a small population (4 million people) that is very homogeneous regarding race, religion, income, educational level, and life experience. Politically, Norway has a social democratic tradition with high emphasis on welfare and equality. A high percentage of Gross National Product is reallocated among individuals and groups through government agencies; and rules and regulations are used to ensure that individuals obtain an acceptable standard of living regardless of individual fortune. Thus, smallness, homogeneity, and equality are important characteristics of the Norwegian society. This is in contrast with the United States, which is characterized by a large heterogeneous population and relatively large differences among people in terms of economic status.

In addition to smallness, homogeneity, and relative equality, three other general characteristics of the Norwegian society are believed to have important implications for conflict management: high income level, strong national identification among people, and importance of informal networks.

Norway has enjoyed a high and rising GNP per capita, surpassing the average income level of the United States. The government has controlled a large portion of total revenues and has allocated it to groups in a way that has buffered the system from conflicts. This has important implications for conflict intensity, as resource scarcity is a major source of conflicts in organized systems (Pfeffer, 1981). When ample resources are available, they can be used to buffer individuals and groups from each other, and thereby reduce the conflict potential. The wealth of the nation combined with government intervention has reduced the frequency of intense conflicts in Norwegian society.

Norway has a fairly isolated geographical location in the northern part of Europe. Although the economy has been very open regarding international trade, people make strong distinctions between Norway and its neighbors. For example, Norwegians see themselves as Norwegians, not as Europeans. This strong group identification has resulted in strong in-group cohesion and some intergroup (i.e., international) skepticism. As we learn from social psychological intergroup theory (Tajfel, 1981), a situation like this usually reduces the intensity of in-group conflicts.

Given the smallness and homogeneity of the nation, informal ties between people in key social positions are easily developed. If they do not know each other personally, they do, at least, know about each other. Social anthropologists use the metaphor of a small village for the Norwegian society (Klausen, 1984). In a small village there is a lot of implicit communication, and informal contacts keep people informed about what is going on. Therefore much communication about conflicts is indirect, and people can relate to the problems without openly confronting the conflict (Barnes, 1954). Furthermore, Norway has a high level of participation in political decisions and many institutions through which such participation is secured (Rokkan, 1968). The high degree of informal contacts and the multiple channels for participative decision-making reduce the intensity of open conflict in the society.

Two institutional factors that relate directly to how conflicts are handled in and between organizations are the *negotiation economy* and the *participative management system*. The organization of economic activities in a society is typically discussed in terms of three different models: a market economy, a planned economy, and a mixed economy. A market economy implies that a large number of sellers and buyers engage in transactions on the basis of price and product information. In a competitive market economy, transactions are made on the basis of information and short-term individual goals. In a planned economy the production and distribution processes are centrally planned through a bureaucratic domination system. In a mixed economy there is a division of labor between the market and the bureaucracy—that is, some activities are taken care of by the market while others are governed by the bureaucracy. In general, the United States is considered to have more of a market economy and Norway to have more of a mixed economy. However, Scandinavian institutional sociologists label the Norwegian system a negotiation economy (Nielsen & Pedersen, 1989). In a negotiation economy important decisions are made through an institutionalized decision process involving political bodies, government agencies, interest groups, and private companies. The system differs from a mixed economy by not having a sharp division of labor between the market and the bureaucracy. Most important decisions are made through a complex negotiation and influence process involving multiple parties. This negotiation process is partly institutionalized, with formal arenas where parties and problems meet (e.g., in centralized wage negotiations), and partly informal, through direct contacts between the small number of actors in an informal network. When the negotiation process is institutionalized, it implies that there are rules and procedures for participation and decision processes. Thus, a negotiation economy functions, in part, because of a well-developed and regulated system of multiparty negotiation.

The dominant American system is a market economy, where the parties can terminate their relationship when they face conflicts. Decisions are, to a large extent, made by the two transaction partners. Politicians, government agencies, and interest groups play minor roles in economic decisions involving private companies. In Norway, on the other hand, a complex negotiation process between multiple actors is an important characteristic of economic organization. This decision process is partly institutionalized through a set of precedents, rules, and regulations. The general tendency is to resolve economic conflicts through forcing (market power) and change of transaction partners in the United States, and through negotiation and institutionalized rules in Norway.

The negotiation economy is not only an integral part of the environment for Norwegian organizations, but it is also institutionalized in the participative management system inside individual organizations. Norway has been in the forefront when it comes to industrial democracy, which has resulted in important labor legislation, action research programs and industrial participation, and a general focus on the quality of work life (Emery & Thorsrud, 1976; Elden, 1978). The result has been strong employee participation in organizational decision-making, and many cooperative activities between workers, unions, and management both at the local company level and through their national associations. In contrast, the United States has a more strictly contractual relationship between employees and the firm, where wages and benefits are exchanged for work and control. As a result, conflicts involving employees will, to a larger extent, be handled through negotiation in Norway than in the United States.

The negotiation economy and the participative management system in Norway foster negotiation as a decision-making mechanism and, thus, negotiation as a dispute management procedure. When we combine the concepts of negotiation economy and participative management with smallness, homogeneity, and equality, we can also say something about decision criteria used in conflict situations. A social comparison process based on procedural and distributive justice becomes important. Different negotiation processes are heavily interlinked, and conflict decisions easily become matters of principle rather than of pragmatic resolution of specific conflicts. Therefore, in wage negotiations, for example, the parties involved in a conflict frequently must look at the larger consequences beyond the specific conflict, and it becomes important to reach consensus decisions.

We propose that national differences in negotiation behavior are predominantly culturally determined. As a framework for understanding cultural differences between Norway and the United States, the empirical work of Hofstede (1980) is the starting point. Hofstede suggests that people have mental programs that are developed through childhood and reinforced through organizational life. This mental program includes beliefs, values, attitudes, expectations, and behavioral tendencies. He argues that shared, or collective, mental programs among people within a nation constitute an important part of the cultural identity of the nation. To obtain information on cultural differences between nations, Hofstede used a survey method, gathering data from employees in a large multinational company in forty nations. The results showed that four cultural dimensions could explain much of the differences among countries: degree of masculinity, degree of individualism, degree of uncertainty avoidance, and degree of power distance.

The major difference between Norway and the United States is on the masculinity dimension. The score for Norway is 8 while the United States has a score of 62. The United States does have a significantly more masculine culture than Norway. In a masculine culture, assertiveness is highly valued, while a feminine culture values cooperation and a friendly atmosphere. There is also a marked difference regarding degree of individualism. The United States has a more individualistic collective mental program than Norway. A high degree of individualism implies a focus on individualistic and extrinsic goals in organizational behavior. In an individualistic culture, there is a general tendency to focus on the individual's autonomy from the organization and on individual accomplishment. There is also a difference between Norway and the United States on power distance, although this difference is smaller. In the United States the power difference between individuals holding different hierarchical positions is more generally accepted than in Norway. There is little difference between the two countries in uncertainty avoidance. In general, the results indicate that Norway has a culture that is less masculine, less individualistic, and more egalitarian (i.e., smaller power distance) than the United States. These results from Hofstede's study have high face validity and complement the conclusions drawn by social anthropologists studying the Norwegian society. We will now discuss the implications of these cultural differences on styles of handling conflicts in negotiation processes.

MANAGERIAL STYLES

When a potential conflict exists, it can be activated through a variety of conflict-management procedures. Typical procedures are rule following, third-party intervention, decoupling, and negotiation. *Rule following* implies that preestablished rules and regulations are used as standards for making decisions in conflict situations. *Third-party intervention* implies that a body outside the conflict relationship becomes involved in resolving the conflict. *Decoupling* implies that the conflicting parties are removed from each other—either by moving individuals to new positions or firing them, or by reorganizing the system such that the interdependence between actors is altered. *Negotiation* implies that the parties themselves handle the conflict through direct contact. These different procedures are used in most national contexts to some extent. We believe there are variations in managerial styles caused by the institutional differences among nations in the frequency of using the different procedures.

Rule following implies that preestablished rules and regulations are used as standards for making decisions in conflict situations. Most observers would say that Norway is a well-regulated society, and there are laws and legislation (e.g., the Work Environment Act) that ensure the rights of workers. An important factor is that the rules and regulations function as formal dispute resolution systems, by ensuring participation and proper conflict handling. In the United States, it seems that rules and regulations do to a larger extent serve as mechanisms for behavior control and as standards for sanctions. Thus, we cannot conclude that rules and regulations are used more or less in Norway than in the United States. The rules simply serve different purposes. While rules in the American system serve as a guide for outcome decisions in conflict episodes, in Norway rules more often serve as a means for securing procedural justice in decision-making. Rules have a process focus to ensure just negotiation in Norway, and have more of an outcome focus in the American system.

In the Norwegian system rules and procedures serve as means to institutionalize conflicts. This may be a functional way of expressing voice (Hirschman, 1970) in a national environment, where interpersonal conflict behavior through open confrontation is not very acceptable. Thus, the Norwegian institutions may substitute for the culturally based American inclinations to confront conflicts through tough distributive behavior and domination as dispute management procedures. For instance, in the private sector 56 percent of Norwegians are organized in trade unions (Fennefoss, 1988). The trade unions handle disputes between employees and employers through institutionalized procedures. In the United States, on the other side, only 17.9 percent of employees are organized and the percentage is declining (Goldfield, 1987). We suggest that many of the conflicts that are handled through institutions in Norway are handled through interpersonal confrontation in the United States.

Thus, with regard to rule following, we put forward two propositions:

Proposition 1: In Norway, rules and regulations to a large extent serve as a formal conflict management procedure, with the purpose of ensuring procedural justice. In the United States, rules and regulations to a larger extent serve as a mechanism for outcome control in organizations.

Proposition 2: In Norway, rules and regulations serve as institutional substitutes for the American cultural inclination of expressing voice through interpersonal confrontation.

Third-party intervention implies that a body outside the conflict relationship becomes involved in resolving the conflict. We can distinguish between formal and informal third-party systems. Informal intervention can take place inside organizations when managers get involved in disputes between individuals and groups at lower organizational levels. In the United States, managers frequently get involved in such conflicts between subordinates (Sheppard, 1984). Managers are expected to be active troubleshooters. In Norwegian organizations, managers are less inclined to involve themselves in disputes when they are not themselves a party in the conflict. When it comes to formal third-party intervention, the situation is somewhat different. In institutionalized conflicts with extensive rules and regulations for conflict handling—such as in wage negotiation—there are typically structured institutions for third-party intervention in the Norwegian system. For instance, the ombudsman system is well developed in Norway to ensure that the interests of less powerful groups have a voice in the decision process. The third-party system is, in such situations, used extensively. In general, the United States has a more developed formal third-party system covering a broader set of conflict situations—for example, in neighborhood disputes, family conflicts, and contractual business disputes. The reason may be that conflicts often become more intensive within the American system, and that penalties for not reaching a joint decision are higher. Based on the above discussion, the following proposition is suggested:

Proposition 3: American managers will to a larger extent than Norwegian managers involve themselves as a third party in disputes among subordinates.

Decoupling implies that the conflicting parties are removed from each other—either by moving individuals to new positions or terminating the employment relationship, or by reorganizing the system such that the interdependence between actors is altered. Both techniques can be used to alter the relationship between the conflicting parties. Removing or transferring individuals because they do not function well in conflict situations are more easily done in the United States than in Norway. In the United States a high degree of mobility is part of organizational life, and organizations have the prerogative of handling individual problems to their liking. In the Norwegian system, the rights of the individual employee are more protected, and management is less inclined to confront individuals. In Norwegian organizations it is therefore easier to reorganize the system in order to change conflictual relations than to move individuals. Consequently, the U.S. system uses decoupling at the individual level more than Norway, while the Norwegian system favors reorganization as a means to overcome conflicts and problems of cooperation. With respect to decoupling, this suggests the following proposition:

Proposition 4: The U.S. system uses transfer of individuals more frequently as a decoupling means than the Norwegian system. The Norwegian system uses reorganization more often as a decoupling means than the U.S. system.

We have argued that Norwegian managers are less likely than American managers to use third-party intervention, decoupling at the individual level, and rules as a basis for sanctions and outcome control. Negotiation is the most preferred dispute management procedure in Norwegian organizations. Negotiation includes any form of conflict management where the parties themselves are responsible for making a joint decision on the conflictive issues through interpersonal contact. The institutional reasons for the tendency to use negotiation frequently are smallness, homogeneity, relative equality, high income level, a negotiation economy, and participative management system. The following proposition is therefore suggested:

Proposition 5: Negotiation, relative to other conflict management procedures, is used more frequently as a conflict-management procedure in Norway than in the United States.

STYLES OF HANDLING INTERPERSONAL CONFLICT

When a potential conflict is channeled into a specific conflict management procedure, the actual process of conflict behavior takes place. In this process there are alternative behavioral styles that can be used even within a specific conflict-management procedure. For example, third-party intervention could be in the form of mediation, inquisitorial intervention, adversarial intervention, or it could be used to provide impetus to the parties to solve the problem themselves. These intervention strategies involve different behavioral strategies and tactics and within each of the intervention methods—for example, in mediation—behavioral tactics may vary significantly among individual mediators (Sheppard, 1984) and cultures.

This chapter will be limited to a discussion of differences among nations in terms of styles in handling interpersonal conflicts in organizations. Rahim (1985) identifies five conflict-handling styles: integrating, obliging, dominating, avoiding, and compromising. Each style can be used more or less forcefully, and it is important to note that all styles might be necessary in conflict management, depending upon the nature of the conflict (Rahim, 1992). In single-issue conflicts, dominating may be the most effective style in producing substantial results for the focal manager if the other party is obliging. Otherwise it may be wise to invite the other party to a give-and-take process (i.e., compromise). In complex negotiations, integrative behavior may be most effective in producing substantial results and in developing good relations between the parties. Finally, avoiding or obliging may be most appropriate if the conflict issue is perceived as insignificant to the person. However, in this chapter, we are not primarily concerned with individual behavioral flexibility but with general behavioral tendencies that can be derived from the national context. Previously we have suggested that cultural factors influence the choice of style in interpersonal conflicts in organizations, and we have outlined how Norway and the United States differ on important cultural dimensions.

Integrating

Integrative behavior implies a concern both for one's own interests and for the interests of the counterpart. Furthermore, it usually requires a fairly intensive problem-solving process where information and interests are shared, issues redefined, and multiple solutions evaluated and developed. Integrative behavior involves a high degree of creativity and joint problem-solving (Pruitt & Rubin, 1986). Integrative behavior is suitable in complex conflict situations where multiple issues are handled simultaneously. This integrative process obviously demands high energy involvement from the parties, and active efforts to satisfy the interests of both parties.

The relative collective nature of the Norwegian culture should indicate an interest in finding solutions that are acceptable to both parties. Furthermore, the lack of assertiveness documented by Norway's position on the masculinity dimension should also facilitate a less competitive and more solution-oriented behavior than in the more masculine American culture. The high value placed on honesty, on the validity of arguments, and on information sharing in Norway should also facilitate integrative behavior. Furthermore, the strong orientation toward reasoning and logical arguments as a basis for decision-making should foster solutions based on interests and facts, rather than on power and strategic maneuvers. Social anthropologists also stress the strong emphasis on procedural justice and social comparison in Norway. A strong symmetrical orientation in exchange relations and a consensus orientation toward other people should foster integrative behavior in Norway. The general conclusion is, therefore, that the Norwegian culture fosters integrative behavior over distributive positional behavior, and a greater degree of integrative behavior than does the American culture.

There are, however, reasons to believe that the integrative orientation in Norway is not as strong as the above arguments would indicate. A lack of willingness to pursue specific goals with vigor may hinder the achievement of integrative solutions in negotiations (Pruitt, 1981), even if the general cultural tendency in Norway would indicate a preference for integrative behavior. The potential for integrative solutions that comes from the willingness to find just solutions may not be reached because of the tendency to avoid confrontation and for a strong consensus orientation. With respect to differences in integrative behavior between the United States and Norway, the arguments suggest the following proposition:

Proposition 6: There is a general tendency for Norwegian managers to use integrative behavior more frequently than American managers. But when American managers use integrative behavior they do so with more force than their Norwegian counterparts.

Obliging

Obliging implies a willingness to sacrifice one's own gains in order to reach settlement in a conflict situation. If the other party initiates joint problem solving through integrative behavior, or signals a willingness to compromise, there is no need for focal persons to sacrifice their own interests by obliging. Obliging, therefore, is most typically a reaction to tough demands made by the other party. Obliging is a complementary style to dominating in a conflict episode.

As suggested above, Norwegians favor decisions based on reasons and logical arguments rather than on power differences and strategic maneuvers. The strong symmetrical orientation in exchange relations should indicate a strong dislike for giving in to demands from a competitive counterpart. We suggest that Norwegians will find a decision procedure where they are expected to oblige to be highly unjust. They will therefore try to change the negotiation situation into integration, or avoid the conflict altogether, rather than give in to the demands of the other party.

In the more individualistic and masculine American culture a stronger acceptance of power differences is expected in organizational systems. Employees will to a larger extent accept the managerial prerogative to make unilateral decisions, and will oblige to the demands of higher level managers within the context of hierarchical organizational systems. Thus, we put forward the following proposition:

Proposition 7: Norwegians, due to the equality orientation, have a strong dislike for obliging in conflict situations, and will oblige less frequently than Americans in organizational conflicts.

Dominating

Domination behavior is the tendency to actively force a preferred solution in a conflict without taking into account the interests of the other party. The focal party takes a tough positional stand on the conflict issue and demands concessions from the other party. Dominating implies a zero-sum conceptualization of conflicts, where the quality of one's own outcome is inversely related to the quality of the outcome for the other party.

Dominating seems not to be typical behavior in Norwegian organizations. Managers generally have a very nonconfrontational style. If at all possible, they do avoid open domination. An anthropologist argues that the ideal for a Norwegian manager is to be invisible! Given the smallness, homogeneity, and equality norm of the population, managers should not separate themselves from the groups they are leading, and they should not dictate subordinate behavior. Thus, domination becomes an unacceptable form of conflict handling. In the United States, hierarchical differences between people in work organizations give the manager the prerogative to dominate. Managers are more or less expected to dominate, otherwise they do not do their job properly. The reason may be the greater heterogeneity, larger size, and higher status differences in the United States compared to Norway. If we move from the interpersonal level inside organizations to the interorganizational level, we find the same pattern. Because of the small number of potential contract partners in the Norwegian business community, a company will have long-term problems if it uses its market power to dominate and force solutions on less powerful actors. In the American marketplace, where there are more actors and potential contractual partners available, powerful companies can use force more easily. They are not so dependent on specific others. Furthermore, given the close links among several actors in the Norwegian negotiation economy, a company must be careful not to lose its goodwill and reputation by dominating other companies. If it uses its power improperly it may be criticized and penalized in the complex negotiation system. Thus, the conclusion seems quite clear: domination is expected to be used more often in the United States than in Norway and it is also more accepted (and even expected) of managers and companies in the United States.

Norwegians are far less comfortable with tough positional behavior than their American counterparts. By examining the Hofstede dimensions the reasons seem obvious. Americans are more comfortable with dominating because of their more assertive inclination (i.e., the masculinity dimension) and their more self-oriented goals (i.e., the individualistic dimension). We therefore put forward the following proposition:

Proposition 8: American managers have a general tendency to use a dominating style in negotiation more frequently and more forcefully than Norwegian managers.

Avoiding

Avoiding is the degree to which the individual withdraws from the conflict episode. Active avoidance behavior involves efforts to cognitively reduce the importance of the potential conflict to trivial matters, to sidestep the conflict, or to postpone the conflict indefinitely.

Avoidance behavior seems to be more frequently used in Norway than in the United States. This can partly be understood by examining the scores on the cultural dimensions. Low degree of masculinity in Norway implies that assertive behavior is not highly accepted, thus individuals are less likely to confront each other. Furthermore, the lower degrees of power distance and individualism indicate that individuals should not separate themselves from others, and should not pursue their own interests openly when they differ from those of other people.

According to anthropologist Gullestad (1984), Norwegians are satisfied with life when they have peace and quiet surroundings. This implies that turbulence and conflicts are seen as uncomfortable and disrupting. Furthermore, Norway has high cultural integration, implying that communication is often implicit and by grapevine. Thus, even if a potential conflict is perceived by the parties and not handled by any procedure other than negotiation, people involved in informal conflicts are often very passive. Anthropologists (e.g., Klausen, 1984) studying Norway also suggest that there is a lack of "social climax" in interpersonal relations. Individuals do have a subdued interpersonal style in which they keep themselves calm, do not overreact, and do not challenge other people. The result is that individuals restrain themselves rather than express their thoughts and feelings. Interpersonal relations at work are mainly task-related and not very expressive and emotional. Conflicts must be task-related and based on logical and just arguments. The result is that it is a burden, both personally and emotionally, to express conflicts, and one therefore tends to avoid them altogether. This avoidance behavior can be in the form of not expressing disagreements and frustrations openly, or in terms of active efforts to postpone the conflict or redefine it into less controversial issues. Thus, both active and passive avoidance behavior is frequently used in the Norwegian culture.

The tendency to avoid conflict is most typical in informal conflict situations. When institutionalized procedures for conflict management exist, a different set of rules applies. In such situations one is not only allowed, but also expected, to play out one's own interests forcefully. It seems, therefore, that institutional procedures are important ritualistic arenas for expressing behavior not usually accepted in everyday working life. America, by contrast, seems to have a higher degree of robustness in expressing conflicts. The culture is more individualistic and results-oriented, and the use of power is more acceptable. This is not to say that avoidance behavior is infrequent in the United States, but only that it is less so than in Norway.

In summary, the above discussion implies that there is a tendency to avoid informal conflicts in Norwegian organizations. Only when conflict procedures are institutionalized is there a degree of comfort with conflicts. The more pluralistic, hierarchical, and individualistic American society facilitates far more active handling of conflict. There is less of a tendency to postpone conflict, or to make it into conflicts over principles through formalized procedures. Thus, we postulate that there is a marked, culturally caused, difference between the United States and Norway in degree of avoidance behavior.

An interesting question is how the tendency to avoid conflicts affects organizational effectiveness and individual well-being. Most textbooks on conflict management postulate that it is important to express conflicts openly in order to achieve both innovation and change, and individual satisfaction and motivation. If these assumptions are correct, Norwegian organizations should have problems regarding both the well-being of individuals and organizational adaptation and development. Individuals may be frustrated because it is difficult to express disagreement. We may find low adjustment because Norwegians avoid uncomfortable confrontations. But the picture is more complicated than this. The tendency to avoid and to postpone conflict may also result in a more mature perspective on the conflicts that are eventually confronted. The decision-making process may be more constructive when the conflicts are channeled into prearranged institutional procedures than when they are handled on an ad hoc basis. The result may also be a more consensus-based outcome than in the more results-oriented American system. It may be that if Norway would adopt the more direct American system, the result would be more destructive power struggles in which interest groups would block any changes. The American openness may be functional in a system with status differences and an individualistic orientation, but less so in the more egalitarian Norwegian setting. Thus, the recommendation in many conflict management textbooks may be culturally specific to the American context and may not apply well in Norway. This discussion suggests the following proposition:

Proposition 9: Norwegian managers have a general tendency to avoid conflicts more often than their American counterparts.

Compromising

A party can take a compromise stand on a conflictive issue by engaging in a give-and-take process. The person will signal a willingness to partly sacrifice one's own interests if the other party is willing to do likewise. Compromising involves a certain degree of gamesmanship, rhetoric, and strategic opportunistic behavior as the parties move from their opening offers toward a compromise solution.

Anthropologists suggest that the Norwegian culture does not foster "gamesmanship" and that Norwegians are not very playful in their behavior. Indeed foreign businesspeople negotiating with Norwegians say that Norwegians are very honest, but also very naive in negotiation situations (Habert & Lillebø, 1988). They are generally reluctant to place their initial offer high above their reservation point and are also careful when it comes to using information strategically. It also follows that rhetoric does not have an important place in the Norwegian culture. Rhetoric is seen more or less as manipulative behavior, and high value is put on honest information, reasonable arguments, and logical thinking. The just solution is highly valued, and solutions that result from positional strategic maneuvers are not very well accepted. In the same way that logic is more important than rhetoric, and justice is more important than power, reason is more important than subjective personal attributes. A negotiation result should therefore come as a result of a contest over the validity of different arguments and not as a result of a positional game. These arguments are, of course, a bit overstated, but the basic proposition is clear: compromise behavior is not very well accepted in Norway. In the United States there is more freedom for individual expression, short-term individual goals are pursued more openly, and toughness and power use are accepted in both interorganizational relations (e.g., business contracts) and in intraorganizational behavior (e.g., individual career pursuit and intergroup conflicts over resource allocation). The proposition on compromising is as follows:

Proposition 10: Compromising is not a very acceptable style of conflict behavior in Norway, and is used less frequently in Norway than in the United States.

A general proposition drawn in the previous section was that Norway is one of the countries that most frequently uses negotiation as a conflict-handling procedure. In this section we suggest that the cultural characteristics of the society make the process of negotiation uncomfortable for the participants, with a resulting low energy involvement in the conflict-management process. A general conclusion is that both conflict-management procedures and behavioral styles used in conflict situations vary between nations because of their different institutional and cultural context. Furthermore, different forms of conflict management may be functional in different national settings. This makes universal and general theories of conflict management difficult to achieve.

It is argued that *compared to the United States* the Norwegian culture tends to foster a higher degree of avoidance behavior, a lower degree of distributive behaviors (i.e., dominating, compromising, and obliging) and a somewhat higher degree of integrative behavior. What are the implications of these differences in terms of constructive conflict management? The normative literature on negotiation is skeptical concerning dominating, basically because it creates difficult interpersonal relations and does not produce high-quality solutions in complex negotiations. But in zero-sum situations dominating and compromising may be superior in generating good substantive results for oneself than any other behavior. In Norway it may be problem that real zero-sum games are not played out properly and it is difficult to get quick solutions on conflictive issues. In the United States the relationship problem potentially created by dominating may not be important because both parties accept dominating. A problem in the United States may be that nonobvious high-quality solutions to conflicts are often not achieved because the parties play out conflicts as competitive struggles over obvious conflict dimensions.

ALTERNATIVE DISPUTE MANAGEMENT

Alternative dispute management procedures are a means used to assist the parties in reaching settlements on conflictive issues. In the dispute management literature a variety of third-party roles (e.g., Goldberg, Green

& Sander, 1985) and institutional channels for productive conflict management (e.g., Ury, Brett & Goldberg, 1988) are identified and discussed.

The most significant uses of alternative dispute management in Norway are in the field of industrial relations and in the use of ombudsmen for a variety of problem areas on the societal level. Alternative dispute management is to a lesser extent used for the handling of specific and informal conflicts within and between organizations.

The Norwegian system of industrial relations is fairly centralized, with intensive cooperation among unions, trade associations, and government. The system has made it possible to link a variety of issues, such as level of taxation and wage increases, in negotiations. Furthermore, the parties have incentives to see beyond short-term goals when settlements on conflicts are drafted. The centralized system is backed up by institutions and procedures for codetermination, mediation, and arbitration at both local and central levels. The institutional channels used for conflict management in industrial relations have resulted in fairly peaceful collaboration. Integrative solutions can be reached because the system design allows for linking issues within specific conflict episodes, and for linking issues over time.

At the societal level the ombudsman role is extensively used. An ombudsman acts as a fact finder and advocate of interests that may otherwise be ignored in decision-making. The ombudsman role is an institutionalized mechanism to ensure that powerful actors cannot ignore legitimate interests and less powerful parties when decisions are made. An ombudsman therefore not only acts as a go-between in conflicts but also as a means of staging conflicts on issues that might otherwise be ignored.

Alternative dispute management also receives increasing attention in disputes traditionally handled (unsuccessfully) by the courts. Examples are counsels established for handling community conflicts and the use of mandatory mediation in divorce negotiations. The development toward alternative dispute management comes from the recognition that traditional dispute management procedures often do not produce stable, high-quality settlements on disputes. Furthermore, as the heterogeneity of the Norwegian society increases, and the general economic recession reduces the opportunities to buffer the system from conflicts by using slack resources, the intensity of conflicts increases. The result is an increasing interest in alternative dispute management procedures as a means of handling conflicts constructively.

Inside specific organizations, and in contractual disputes between organizations, alternative dispute management procedures are not frequently used. This may be due to the general preference for direct integrative negotiation and avoidance as conflict-handling styles in the Norwegian society. When the actors themselves must establish procedures for third-party intervention, they are reluctant to do so owing to the normative orientation toward direct negotiation and collaboration.

DISCUSSION

In this section we draw some cross-cultural implications from the previous discussion, and we outline some theoretical and managerial implications. Making cross-cultural inferences about behavior is dangerous because one will assume that individuals involved in cross-cultural conflict management and negotiation actually represent the national stereotypes. This is unreasonable, because individual behavior deviates more or less from this standard, and also because individuals engaged in cross-cultural conflict management may have an experience that hinders national tendencies to dominate. For instance, the most international industrial sectors in Norway are shipping and oil. In both these industries there are industry-specific cultural traditions that reduce the influence of national differences when conflict situations are confronted.

If we assume that the stereotypical American ways to manage conflicts are played out against the stereotypical Norwegian conflict management style, we get some interesting implications. First, Americans will be more likely to use domination and decoupling, while Norwegians would prefer negotiations. For an American subsidiary in Norway with Norwegian employees, for example, the differences in preferred ways of handling conflicts may create problems. Norwegians will find the procedures less acceptable in the Norwegian context. The result may be a conflict over principles that is channeled into more formal institutionalized conflict procedures. The choice of conflict management procedures and conflict behavior may also negatively affect the organizational culture, and the potential for cooperation between employer and employees may be reduced. Americans, on the other hand, will probably feel frustrated and impatient because of their inability to achieve results and because of a threat toward their management prerogatives. The final result may be an adjustment on both sides where the American tendency to dominate is reduced somewhat, and where Norwegian organizations and employees must accept more limited influence in the organization. The Norwegian oil industry, with many American companies involved, has, in fact, during its early years experienced a development similar to the one just described.

The Norwegian method of channeling potential conflicts into institutionalized procedures, and of using extensive employee participation and negotiation rather than other decision procedures, may also face problems within an American context. A Norwegian subsidiary in the United States may, for example, find itself unable to activate the employees in a way necessary for a participative system to function.

This discussion indicates that it is difficult to transfer conflict-management procedures and behavior across national boundaries, and that cross-cultural management becomes difficult when the preferred behavior is different in the two countries. The next question is how the negotiation process itself is affected when the two cultural stereotypes meet. This will be relevant when contracts between companies from the two countries are negotiated. The United States is an important market for many Norwegian companies, and negotiation with American counterparts are therefore important for many Norwegian managers. The previous discussion clearly indicates that the Americans will be more forceful, results-oriented, positional, and strategic in their behavior than their stereotypical Norwegian counterparts. The Norwegians will be more reason-oriented and less "playful." The result may be that the American becomes impatient with a less active Norwegian counterpart, and the Norwegian may become frustrated with the more forceful and less "polite" American style. The result may be a difficult negotiation climate where common rules of the game are difficult to establish. Therefore it may be difficult to get good substantial results, develop trust, and to ensure good long-term relations.

A final question may be who wins the conflict over negotiation style. In general there seems to be a tendency for distributive styles to win over more integrative styles. If the Norwegians are not comfortable with the more positional game and are not willing to play it strategically, they may easily lose out to the Americans.

The dominant research on conflict management is American. In the American literature a heavy focus is put on negotiation as a conflict-handling procedure and on integration as the superior negotiation strategy. In this chapter we have suggested that this emphasis may be more normative than descriptive. We have proposed that the stereotypical American way to manage conflicts, at least compared to Norway, is through forcing, decoupling, and intervention as dispute management procedures, and to use tough distributive behavior when they negotiate. Norwegians are more inclined to use negotiation as a conflict-handling procedure, and to negotiate less forcefully than their American counterparts. The propositions put forward in this chapter suggest that institutional and cultural factors are important determinants of how conflicts are managed. Empirical research is needed to describe variations in conflict behavior caused by cultural differences, and to develop universal theoretical framework for conflict management.

While the different conflict-management styles have institutional and cultural causes, and their effectiveness to some extent is context-specific, there are interesting implications for management training and conflict research. The training implications for Norwegian and American managers will be different. For Americans the heavy emphasis in the literature (e.g., Fisher & Ury, 1981) on negotiation and integrative behavior seems reasonable. For Norwegians more emphasis should be put on other conflict-management procedures and behavioral styles in order to increase their behavioral repertoire, on dominating and compromise behavior to be used in zero-sum situations, and on being more forceful in integrative negotiation situations. In general, both Americans and Norwegians should expand their behavioral repertoire, and increase their behavioral flexibility, so that they are able to vary their conflict-handling procedures and behavioral strategies and tactics according to the nature of the conflict (Rahim, 1992) and the cultural context of the process.

The theoretical implications are basically related to empirical verification of national differences in conflict behavior. This can partly be done by comparative experimental research. Furthermore, there is a need for field research in similar settings of conflicts where actual behavioral styles in conflict management can be compared. Furthermore, cross-cultural research should be developed by comparing results when, for example, American subjects are pitted against Norwegian subjects. Finally, the cultural contingency factor should be taken more seriously in theory development, in empirical research, and when normative behavioral recommendations are made.

REFERENCES

Barnes, J. M. (1954). Class and committees in a Norwegian island parish. *Human Relations, 7*, 15–25.

Brett, J., & Rognes, J. (1986). Intergroup relations. In P. Goodman (Ed.), *Designing effective work groups* (pp. 202–236). San Francisco: Jossey-Bass.

Elden, M. (1978). *Three generations of work democracy experiments in Norway: Beyond classical sociotechnical analysis*. Trondheim, Norway: IFIM Report.

Emery, F. E., & Thorsrud, E. (1976). *Democracy at work*. Leiden: Martinus Nijhoff.

Fennefoss, A. (1988). *Lønnstaker-organisering* [Organized labor]. Oslo: FAFO Report.

Fisher, R., & Ury, W. (1981). *Getting to yes: Negotiating agreement without giving in*. Boston: Houghton-Mifflin.

Goldberg, S., Green, E., & Sander, F. (1985). *Dispute resolution*. Boston: Little, Brown.

Goldfield, M. (1987). *The decline of organized labor in the United States*. Chicago: University of Chicago Press.

Gullestad, M. (1984). *Kitchen table society*. Oslo: Norwegian University Press.

Habert, K., & Lillebø, A. (1988). *Made in Norway: Norwegians as others see them*. Oslo: Norwegian School of Management Press.

Hirschman, A. O. (1979). *Exit, voice and loyalty*. Cambridge, MA: Harvard University Press.

Hofstede, G. (1980). *Culture's consequences: International differences in work-related values*. Beverly Hills, CA.: Sage.

Klausen, A.M (Ed.). (1984). *Den Norske væremåte* [The Norwegian conduct]. Oslo: Cappelen.

Nielsen, K., & Pedersen, O. (1989). *Forhandlingsøkonomi i Norden* [Negotiation economy in Scandinavia]. Oslo: Tano.

Pfeffer, J. (1981). *Power in organizations*. Boston: Pitman.

Pruitt, D. (1981). *Negotiation behavior*. New York: Academic Press.

Pruitt, D., & Rubin, J. (1986). *Social conflict, escalation, stalemate, and settlement*. New York: McGraw-Hill.

Rahim, A. (1985). A strategy for managing conflict in complex organizations. *Human Relations, 36*, 81–89.

Rahim, A. (1992). *Managing conflict in organizations* (2nd ed.). Westport, CT: Praeger.

Rokkan, S. (1968). Norway, numerical democracy and corporate pluralism. In R. Dahl (Ed.), *Political oppositions in Western democracies* (pp. 48–62). New Haven, CT: Yale University Press.

Sheppard, B. (1984). Third party conflict intervention: A procedural framework. In B. M. Staw & L. L. Cummings (Eds.), *Research in organization behavior* (Vol. 6, pp. 141–190). Greenwich, CT: JAI Press.

Tajfel, H. (1982). Social psychology of intergroup relations. *Annual Review of Psychology, 33*, 1–39.

Tjosvold, D. (1989). *Managing conflicts*. Minneapolis: Team Media.

Ury, W., Brett, J., & Goldberg, S. (1988). *Getting disputes resolved: Designing systems to cut the costs of conflict*. San Francisco: Jossey-Bass.

6

SOUTH AFRICA

Frank M. Horwitz

Competitive relationships and a legacy of adversarialism have typified intergroup and interpersonal conflicts in South African (S.A.) organizations. The apartheid legacy has left a divided and wounded society. This chapter examines the relationship between this legacy, sociocultural and economic factors, and prevailing ways of handling conflict in South African organizations. Recent factors reducing the tendency toward authoritarian management styles are explored and the contribution of an array of alternative dispute management organizations is discussed. Future research questions around the coexistence of various conflict-handling styles are proposed.

SOCIAL, CULTURAL, AND ECONOMIC FACTORS

South Africa is a developing multicultural society with structural discrepancies in wealth and opportunity. It has inherent conflicts of interest between and within groups in organizational settings. In 1948 apartheid constitutionally segregated racial groups and banned black access to political, civic, and labor rights. The population of South Africa is 35 million. Some 28 million black people were formally excluded from equal education and employment opportunities until apartheid laws were repealed in the post-1990 period. The apartheid legacy has resulted in over 60 percent of the economically active black population having a primary school education or none at all. An important contemporary issue in this regard is the process of equalizing opportunities and wealth distribution for historically disadvantaged people. Social and economic discrimination date back to 1652 when the first Dutch settlers arrived in the Cape, although it was constitutionally enforced only in 1948, when the Nationalist party came to power. A negotiating process at various levels in South Africa has now begun, but is not an end in itself. Heightened expectations both politically and economically have not been met. Protracted political negotiations aimed at creating a new constitution have not delivered tangible gains at organizational and individual levels in the short term for black people, or security and the protection of rights for whites and other minorities. Conflict inherent in the interaction between individuals and groups cannot be resolved, but rather constructively accommodated or institutionalized (Van der Merwe et al., 1988). This does require structural change and an associated relative or near-power balance between groups. Van der Merwe (1989) refers to the emergence of a "pragmatic flexibility," which can supersede rigid ideological commitment.

Power distance (Hofstede, 1980) and various manifestations of conflict in organizations may be better understood in relation to overall power relations in S.A. society (Foster 1986). Several studies of labor control in mining and industry (Gordon, 1977; Jubber, 1979; Keenen, 1984; & Moodie, 1980) have shown that the hierarchical structure of organizations mirrors that of the wider society with management positions still predominantly white. This occurs within a context of a high degree of centralized economic power. Six groups of companies (Anglo American Corporation, Anglovaal, Liberty Holdings, Rembrandt, Sanlam, and the S.A. Mutual) control 84 percent of the total S.A. market (Savage, 1987). Savage argues that a concomitant increase in interlocking directorships among top companies and a concentration of ownership indicates a significant centralization of economic decision-making in a few hands. Not only is there a shortage of skilled people in South Africa, but a structural inequality in the skills profile occurs. Only 3 percent of 85,000 black matriculants in 1988 had mathematics as a subject. Issues of "legitimacy" and "equity" in the exercise of economic power and managerial authority become problematic when the majority of economic participants are marginal to the economic process. The potential for conflict is exacerbated as individual disempowerment is predominantly on the basis of racial exclusion, and is redressed only indirectly through collective mobilization by trade unions. Less than 10 percent of company directors in South Africa are black. The demands for upward mobility and economic ownership and control have, however, become insistent. It has been argued that through negotiation and compromise the trade union movement has become an effective and legitimate fact of the process of black empowerment (Van der Merwe & Odendaal, 1990).

While white control over many institutions and systems that shaped S.A. society is slipping, there is a crisis of meaning for a large number of black people, a serious alienation from the norms and practices in the white world. The traditional African cultural value of *Ubuntu*, or humaneness, has been eroded with the atomized and often violent existence in township ghettos. Hofstede's (1980) study of work-related attitudes across a wide range of cultures found that S.A. employees tended toward individualism rather than a collective social framework. Urbanization and modernity have reduced the tight social frameworks that characterize collectivist cultures. The migrant labor process has also undermined the unity and cohesion of an extended family tradition in rural areas. Hofstede also found a large power distance between members of S.A. organizations. The power distance phenomenon concerning perceived inequalities in power is an important variable in explaining the high level of conflict in South Africa.

Political and criminal violence has escalated since 1990, in the competition between rival political and ethnic groups for power. Particular problems and tensions have been neglected in the preoccupation with apartheid. Areas of conflict that can be identified and cannot necessarily be resolved constitutionally include racism and multiculturalism; the psychological and socioeconomic effects of urbanization and modernization; heightened expectations in education and training following decades of discrimination and neglect; and inappropriate styles of handling interpersonal conflict and labor management conflict. Van der Merwe and Odendaal (1990, p. 17) conclude that many of these new sources of conflict increasingly cut across racial divides.

In analyzing conflict in S.A. organizations, Bluen (1986) argues that materialist theories tend to disregard behavioral variables. They emphasize broad analytical frameworks rather than individual or work group behavior, and collective rather than interpersonal relations. Until recently, the psychological consequences of conflict in organizations have been largely ignored (Bluen & Fullagar, 1986). Role ambiguity and conflict among shop stewards and industrial relations specialists have received some empirical treatment (Horwitz, 1990). Industrial psychologist S. Bluen (1986) has identified factors and symptoms associated with workplace stress in South Africa. His findings support Hofstede's dimensions in respect to South Africa.

It is possible for different conflict-handling approaches to be applied, depending on the nature of the particular issues on the agenda and their perceived importance to future needs and relationships. However, the process of conflict management in South Africa is particularly fragile. Extraparliamentary reliance on protest politics as a result of historic powerlessness has made way for more open political activity with the unbanning of the African National Congress (ANC) and the release of Nelson Mandela and other political prisoners. However, despite a highly politicized climate, with the Congress of South African Trade Unions (COSATU) and the National Council of Trade Unions (NACTU) being at the forefront of political change, particularly in the 1980s, negotiated compromise on labor issues is widespread. The union movement has gained considerable negotiating experience, albeit mainly of a competitive type. It will be interesting to observe whether the union movement, in turn, will itself become an integral part of creating a climate for reconciliation and integrating styles, not only on conflicts of interest but also in acknowledging both differing and common needs. With black people having labor rights without a concomitant political franchise, the political vacuum created by this paradox was filled by the union movement in the 1980s. While the political space has now developed for unbanned organizations, the trade union movement continues to play an important role in negotiations at both organizational and political levels.

A mutually acknowledged need for interaction may result in conflict accommodation. The grudging realization of mutual interdependence between white and black South Africans after centuries of social and legal separation is slowly drawing South Africans closer together, although serious deep-rooted conflicts remain. The development of common organizational and national symbols across race and cultural groups is both a fundamental process in negotiations and also an important potential outcome of organizational change programs and a reduction in power distance. Giliomee (1990) argues that conflict will not be removed by what he states as the exaggerated influence of stabilization through material benefits. He argues that members of an ethnic minority cannot be placated by improved living standards, but only by an acceptable standing within the political economy and the organization. Giliomee argues further that the acquisition of a "legitimate place in the economy" was a primary reason for Afrikaner ethnic mobilization in the 1930s and 1940s, and that there is little reason to doubt why people of other ethnic groups should not be driven by similar concerns. Department of Manpower statistics indicate that the proportion of Africans, Asians, and colored people in high-level management positions rose from 1.7 percent in 1965 to 6.0 percent in 1985. In the early 1990s there are fewer than 8 percent Africans, Asians, and coloreds in managing director positions according to official statistics. Upward mobility is occurring, albeit slowly.

The status acquired from a meaningful organizational stakeholding and control is limited by the maintenance of social closure and organizational hegemony by whites. An important source of organizational conflict, according to Giliomee, is white worker alienation. Studies (Human & Icely, 1989; Human & Pringle, 1986), point to the extent of white worker disaffection. Human and Pringle found that only 20 percent of white workers held a positive view of the increasing promotion of blacks up the occupational structure. Both studies found that only 20 percent of white workers were "unconcerned" about changing labor patterns. A recent study reported by Giliomee found that 41 percent of white middle management felt that black management appointments were window-dressing. A full 90 percent were opposed to "reverse discrimination." These studies suggest that resistance to change and a concern about tokenism have serious conflict potential in the 1990s. Poor race relations, power distance, and resulting polarization between groups are also affected by a second issue— namely, the demand for occupational mobility of black people, particularly into skilled and managerial positions. A third demand relates to developing an increased sense of involvement in both the job and organization through workers' participation, democratic and consultative styles of leadership, and through financial participation such as share ownership. Research findings in South Africa suggest that up until recently, managerial assumptions tended to be based on Taylorist scientific management approaches to employees, especially in the mining industry (Bluen & Fullagar, 1986). These sources of conflict, however, pose an opportunity for positive and dynamic interventions for organization change, as participation is also a method for inducing cooperative attitudes (Zaleznik, 1990).

The socially and politically fragmented nature of S.A. society offers few unifying symbols of a common national destiny or organizational commitment. Different national anthems and flags reflect the fragmentation of a divided society. Systems have been designed to keep people apart and emphasis has been put on differences rather than building a common destiny. It is in this context that managerial styles and styles of handling interpersonal conflicts are considered.

MANAGERIAL STYLES

Positive and constructive aspects of power in promoting managerial and organization effectiveness have been suggested (Kanter, 1977; Kipnis, 1976; McClelland & Boyatziz, 1982). The dynamics and outcomes of the use of power may depend on whether organizational members believe that their goals are cooperative or competitive (Tjosvold, 1981). In Africa, the values of a democratic culture embody tolerance (the African tenet of *Ubuntu*, humaneness), statesmanship in leaders representing organizations in negotiations, and the importance of mandated representatives. Managerial styles and white attitudes have, however, tended to be based on scientific management assumptions that managers do the thinking and planning and workers do as they are told (Human & Icely, 1987). Associated managerial styles increase power distance in organizations. White managerial assumptions about employees, particularly black workers, frequently cause managers to doubt the ability of these workers to take on higher level responsibilities. Benevolent authoritarianism and paternalism are prevalent, yet effective conflict resolution requires empowerment and a psychological readiness for change (Adam, 1990). Conflict and negotiation in S.A. organizations deal with equity in treatment at the interpersonal level. These issues elicit debate about the very nature of the firm itself. Managerial culture in South Africa is premised on meritocratic values. "Survival of the fittest" notions are examples of Hofstede's individualism. Caution should be exercised on the use of conflict resolution models that may be culturally inappropriate given prevailing managerial styles. Models of conflict resolution require agreement on both the means and ends of conflict resolution. Both collective and interpersonal conflicts have often left a legacy of deep wounds in South Africa.

Win-win integrating styles assume a degree of perceived equality between individuals and seek to get individuals or parties to develop their own mutually acceptable agreements. Benevolent authoritarianism is not compatible with an integrating conflict resolution mode. The "new" South African organization will therefore be exciting and challenging, but also problematic with deep conflicts requiring skillful mediation. A political solution will not necessarily address organizational conflicts. Grass-roots reconciliation is vital too. This will require a paradigm shift for most managers away from the scientific management tradition toward an open, participative style.

This suggests a holistic managerial approach in societies characterized by intense and complex conflicts. In a culture premised on high power distance, individualism, and masculinity, compromise is seen as a weakness in managerial behavior. This is especially relevant when considering styles in handling interpersonal conflict, dealt with elsewhere in this chapter. However, the willingness to compromise on issues is fundamental, but often the real interests of the parties may not be apparent (Fisher & Ury, 1988). A reliance on positional bargaining is common in South Africa. It reflects adversarial and combative managerial behavior. It may produce an agreement, though it may not be a wise one. At various levels of conflict in South Africa, including the organizational level, facilitation is increasingly used. In some organizations, such as PG Bison, this had helped to create a managerial awareness of the consequences of inappropriate assumptions, associated styles, and their impact on the way in which conflict is dealt. Facilitation has been particularly helpful in bringing conflicting groups together—for example, trade unionists, right-wing political organizations, employers, and black political and civic organizations—in the Middleburg forum in which a large steel and alloys firm facilitated a broad-based initiative in conflict intervention. This has resulted in greater understanding and tolerance by managers of the complexity of conflicts around them and a willingness to problem-solve around needs rather than bargain on issues. This is similar to Fisher and Ury's (1981) contention that ascertaining underlying rather than expressed interests is fundamental to a "principled negotiation." These principles are relevant where fundamental inequalities in resources and organizational opportunities also mask deep-rooted human needs and a large power distance.

STYLES OF HANDLING INTERPERSONAL CONFLICT

Integrating

Dostal and Osler (1990) have found that there are a small but increasing number of business organizations in South Africa that have begun creative organization renewal strategies to improve internal relationships and influence their external environment. They refer in this context to Senge and Kiefer's (1984) notion of the metanoic organization, described as an organization that operates under extreme pressure, including deep-rooted conflicts in its external environment, but that consistently achieves high levels of performance. Integrating interpersonal styles, participation, and development of individuals and groups within the organization results in a constructive and mature relationship. Emdin (1990) also notes that there are companies in South Africa (such as Woolworths) that consistently experience lower levels of conflict with employees than the industries in which they work, and they resolve interpersonal conflicts more speedily. Organizations such as Shell Oil, African Explosives and Chemical Industries, Cape Cabinets, and Tongaat-Hullets appear to take a long-term approach and conduct on-going planning on their future direction, with this process becoming part of the internal culture. These organizations focus on trying to optimize interdependencies among employees and managers, with a strong definition of the corporate vision and values. Exploratory studies suggest increasing though still tentative evidence of a shift from domination toward integrating styles at organization and interpersonal levels (Human & Horwitz, 1992). For many of the indigenous peoples of Africa, etiquette associated with the form and nature of interpersonal relations is accorded high value. Mutual respect is extremely important (Blunt, 1985). Many ethnic groups in Africa are, according to Blunt, taught to value courtesy and respect for others.

Labor negotiations are increasingly giving attention to ensuring a fairer distribution of earnings in the nonwage part of agreements on issues such as employment equity, occupational mobility, housing, job grading, pensions, productivity, training, and development. The National Union of Metalworkers of South Africa (NUMSA) has, for example, recently emphasized a training policy aimed at upgrading the skills of unskilled and semiskilled workers. These issues have become increasingly important for trade unions. In dealing with them, an integrating conflict management style has proved viable. As cooperative relationships and optimizing interdependence and common ground are so crucial in South Africa, it is axiomatic that a needs-based, integrating style has validity, but this style is incompatible with authoritarian behavior and paternalism. Yet cooperation and problem solving are fundamental in reducing large power inequalities.

Obliging and Avoiding

Obliging and avoiding are considered together, not because they are necessarily similar, but because there is a paucity of micro-level research data on their prevalence in South Africa. Anecdotal evidence and the author's experience suggest that both occur with some frequency at the supervisor-employee interface. Often a supervisor will avoid dealing with a problem because he or she feels an employee (especially if a union representative) intends bypassing him or her to refer the matter to a higher level. Supervisors are invariably the "ham between the sandwich," being pressured from above and below. A fear of a backlash from employees does result in avoidance of conflict, thus allowing someone more senior to deal with it. Similarly, this insecure and often marginalized feeling also results in an overeagerness to appease, and an obliging style occurs without necessarily resolving the conflict. Hofstede's work would tend not to support a high prevalence of these styles, with South Africa tending toward the weak uncertainty avoidance but high-power distance ends. Not surprisingly in a generally authoritarian society, there is a strong masculinity dimension.

Dominating

Authoritarianism is deeply woven into the fabric of social relations in South Africa, which inclines to the masculine and individualism ends of Hofstede's axes. A survey of COSATU trade unionists shows that 67 percent of respondents saw managers and employees as having few common interests (Maller, 1988). Historically, workplace relations have been perceived as revealing dominating management styles. With more worker influence in the 1980s, a greater willingness to compromise evolved. Certain styles and methods of conflict intervention are situationally contingent. However, dominating styles still remain extensive in interpersonal conflicts in SA organizations, with grudging compromises often being reached. Rahim (1990) emphasizes that the mix and interactive nature of conflict styles is important and that a single-dimensional cooperative-competitive dichotomy may be limited. He argues that certain styles such as compromising and integrating are independent of each other. He highlights the need to acknowledge and learn a flexible mix of styles to deal with different types of conflict in terms of a contingency theory of conflict management. Prevalence of dominating styles is also supported by relatively large power distance in S.A. organizations. A move away from a legacy of authoritarianism and dominating styles of conflict management to integrative and compromise conflict modes at organizational and interpersonal levels seems to be gradually emerging.

Compromising

While the integrative, win-win model is clearly important in creating a constructive climate for interpersonal relations, conflicts over both interests and rights associated with the historical maldistribution of wealth and opportunity in South Africa suggest that (adversarial) compromise bargaining is a feature of management and shop steward relationships at the micro level. However, a shift in the power balance between groups requires a process of healing and reconciliation to overcome the legacy of bitterness, mistrust, and "habituated adversarialism." Such compromise outcomes tend to occur as a result of pressure, rather than natural inclination of individual managers. Power distance encourages the use of power tactics to achieve ends. A reactive emphasis on labor relations fire-fighting and the associated win-lose adversarial tradition of legal remedies to conflict has been a characteristic of employee relations during the 1980s and early 1990s. This inhibits a strategic emphasis on human development and consciously planned organization change and raises the issue of whether integrating and compromising conflict styles can coexist, contingent on the nature of conflict and desired outcomes. Organizational development processes are more compatible with integrative problem solving. However, commitment to outcomes is dependent on the nature of the process. The process, the styles of managers, and the climate in which they interact with employees have a fundamental impact on future relationships. Compromising styles have become more prevalent in negotiations on organizational changes in South Africa for two reasons. First, the years of racial polarization make such a negotiation style seem inevitable. Second, there are insistent demands for a redress of past grievances and inequities. Some even demand retaliation and retribution. These are expressed at organizational levels in manager-worker interaction.

ALTERNATIVE DISPUTE MANAGEMENT

Creativity, tolerance, and flexibility are important ingredients in multicultural settings, if the peaceful and cooperative coexistence of self-associating groups is to occur. At grass-roots levels a variety of initiatives in bridge building and facilitation between groups in conflict have been taken. The training of both labor and community mediators has increasingly occurred through organizations such as the Independent Mediation Service of South Africa (IMSSA) and the Centre for Intergroup Studies (CIS) at the University of Cape Town. The South African Society for Conflict Intervention (SAACI) was launched in 1989. There have also been calls for the formation of a national mediation service (Van der Merwe, 1988), and moves have been made in this direction by the development of a program for training negotiators and mediators. The first national committee of the South African Association of Mediators (SAAM) was also elected in 1989. There are increasing numbers of organizations that could be described as working in the broad field of conflict mediation.

Contributing organizations also include (1) business-based groupings— for example, pressure groups such as the Urban Foundation, (2) church-based groups such as the South African Council of Churches, and (3) interorganizational alliances or citizen initiatives, which attempt to bring people of different views together for seminars and discussion. The Institute for a Democratic Alternative for South Africa (IDASA) is an example. There are also some government-sponsored programs, and academic, educational, and research groups that provide forums for analysis and discussion on conflict issues. Examples of the latter include the South African Institute for Race Relations, and the Centre for Policy Research of the University of the Witwatersrand. A number of other organizations such as the Quakers are making an important contribution to peace work. Some universities have also introduced courses on conflict resolution. The Consultative Business Movement and IDASA emerged in the 1980s to create a dialogue between important interest groups and individuals including the then-banned ANC. The beginning of the 1990 decade has seen these initiatives continue.

The demand for upward occupational mobility by black employees and women has moved into the collective bargaining arena in most industries. In some cases it has been dealt with through negotiation, though there are examples of third-party (industrial court) arbitration on pay discrimination (Sentrachem case). Resistance to change occurs at all levels of an organization, but it is particularly pronounced at the white supervisor and black employee interface. White supervisors frequently have a low level of education, and may have enjoyed job security and sheltered employment, especially in the public sector. Their political inclinations are conservative and they find the sociopolitical changes sweeping South Africa anathema. Deep-rooted racial prejudice, ingrained over generations and socially reinforced by an immediate circle of friends, peers, and family, is a feature at this level of the organization. Interracial conflict and tension are most visible at this level, and the most enlightened employers have not been immune. Employers such as African Explosives and Chemical Industries (AECI) who have made progress in black advancement have often experienced the paradox of white supervisor fear and resistance to change and the heightened expectations of immediate gains both materially and vocationally by black employees.

Recognition "agreements" institutionalize basic worker rights. They have become important mechanisms for regulating industrial conflict since 1979. These agreements frequently provide for negotiated dispute resolution procedures and, more recently, have also included the use of mediation and private arbitration as part of this process. In 1983 a private mediation and subsequently private arbitration service was made available through IMSSA, which provides a resource service to collective bargaining. The use of IMSSA's services has enhanced control by unions and employers of the negotiating process and its outcome, for it has limited government interference or the use of the legalism of the courts. The increased use of mediation is reflected in the fact that in 1984, only 39 mediations occurred, while over 480 occurred annually from 1989 to 1991. Private arbitrations through IMSSA increased from 5 in 1984 to 194 in 1988 and 200 in 1989 (Nupen & Steadman, 1989).

The exposure of employers and unions to collective bargaining over the last decade seems to have largely eradicated misgivings about third-party interventions and has enhanced its value as a resource to collective bargaining. IMSSA provides a service (called relationships by objectives) to assist both parties equally to manage their relationship better and to address conflicts. In South Africa, wage disputes tend to go to mediation, while discipline and dismissal disputes to arbitration, although strict demarcations between disputes of interests and rights are becoming "blurred" with respect to appropriate dispute resolution procedures. Through the development of private mediation and arbitration, an important educational role is also performed with respect to reinforcing the importance of rights associated with the collective bargaining process. A legitimate and credible dispute resolution process is vital in reinforcing the process of enterprise conflict resolution.

DISCUSSION

There is in South Africa a threat of erosion of approaches based on compromise models by human resources philosophies, ideologically trying to "win the hearts and minds" of workers. This is evidenced by a focus away from competitive centralized relations to flexible and decentralized management and employee involvement in industries such as packaging. Employers are increasingly concerned with facilitating decentralized, organization-level improvements in economic/productivity objectives by trying to reduce a large power distance and enhance commitment to organizational objectives. Employee involvement schemes have therefore assumed greater prominence. This shift of managerial strategies to the decentralized level seeks to reduce the competitive relationship patterns of collective bargaining and enhance integration and trust by direct communication with employees, integrating interpersonal styles and union avoidance policies. In this sense, trends in developed and developing countries show similar patterns. Hofstede's research, although using a small single-company data set in South Africa, has a strong face validity. There is scope for further research that incorporates the diversity of culture in South Africa organizations more rigorously. A fundamental question in this regard concerns the feasibility of the coexistence in a single organization of the five-style framework used in this book. The potential for coexistence is to a large extent a function of variables affecting prevailing power realities, including economic factors, changing values, technological advancement, and labor market patterns.

Conflict management requires a reorientation that considers the prospects for "pragmatic flexibility"—a synergy of various forms of conflict management. This relates to Greiner and Schein's (1988) view that a pluralistic/political model is more reflective of organizational realities than rational/bureaucratic or collegial/consensus models. Integrating activities seek a reduction of dominating styles of managements and power distance, although they may introduce a different form of control. Greater participation of employees in decisions affecting their interests may complement compromise-orientated negotiations and procedural resolution of labor relations disputes. Hence, the contextual copresence of integrating and compromising styles within the same organization, together with other situationally appropriate styles of conflict management, is relevant.

The shift toward decentralization of organizational decision-making processes and plant- or enterprise-level participation does not, however, reflect a profound change in power distance and influence in organizations. As organizations decentralize, they tend to centralize certain policy and control functions. In general, it would seem that policy development is formulated centrally, but greater freedom is being granted regarding operationalization of policies, and values, at lower levels. Similarly, broad policy parameters and monitoring controls may tend to be centrally formulated even in operationally decentralized organizations.

The management of organizational change requires internalization of conflict management processes. Organizational responses to social change may be adaptive or transformative, seeking to influence the strategic alignment between internal and external organizational demands. Given the link between management styles and conflict, we can accept that some changes would reduce the potential for conflict (Emdin, 1990). The issue of differing values is associated with conflict resolution processes. An intervening variable that may influence the direction of conflict and values is the desired relationship the parties require. It is postulated that multicultural societies such as South Africa have individualist and collectivist tendencies in various groups. Relationships include collective employer-union interaction, and also the quality of interpersonal relationships between a manager and employee, between peers, and between supervisors and shop stewards. Interpersonal relations may in turn relate to the quality of collective, intergroup relationships.

Conflict arises from both relationship issues and fairness in treatment and substantive issues around pay and conditions of employment. Conflict in S.A. organizations occurs in a social and organization context of dramatic and indeed traumatic change for many people. A holistic focus on organizational change strategies implies that an emphasis needs to be placed on genuine employee involvement and empowerment in areas in which a contribution is possible. Work redesign and both direct and indirect participation are important processes that create meaning in organizational life. Competitive conflict resolution and the associated emphasis on the creation of rights has had a dominant emphasis in organizational decision-making in the 1980s. Collaborative direct forms of employee involvement, and integrating styles with largely performance and job redesign goals, to provide greater personal growth, have become more prominent in organizations such as AECI in the chemical industry and PG Bison. Binnedell (1990) argues that a key question concerning the future of organizations in the private sector is how to prepare businesses to be productive and effective in a transition to a nonracial democratic society, which may tend toward the collectivism dimension. The high concentration of ownership in the hands of a small part of society creates, in some sectors such as beer brewing and distribution, oligarchic trading conditions and power distance internally. Structural inequalities in wealth and opportunity form the basis of intense competitive bargaining in industries such as mining. This underlines the proposition that the mix between integrating and competing styles is variable and indeed fragile in times of deep-rooted conflict.

There is clearly a broad scope for conflict management at several levels, including labor/management relations and intergroup and interpersonal relationship building at organizational levels. Negotiation and conciliation are not part of the historical fabric of S.A. society. The development of democratic structures requires a simultaneous evolution of a tolerant culture in which various forms of conflict management become almost custom or routine. An understanding of the nature of intergroup conflict cannot view race as the sole cause of tensions (Van der Merwe, 1988). While it has undeniably been a fundamental ideological pillar of the apartheid system, the removal of racial discrimination may reduce, but not eliminate, conflict arising from power distance and the pursuit of individualist ends within and between organizations. Social, structural, and economic inequalities may indeed persist in an "apartheid free" South Africa. New alliances, changing patterns of conflict arising from economic disadvantage, and ideological divisions within groups may cut across the traditional racial divide. A paucity of research exists on styles of handling interpersonal conflict in South Africa. In particular, considerable work is needed on the extent to which obliging and avoiding styles occur and the circumstances prevalent. Research in South Africa tends to focus on labor-relations-style characteristics, in particular integrative and compromise approaches (Anstey, 1991). Dogmatic adherence to entrenched positions limits creative and innovative conflict-handling outcomes. These lessons have been learned in the labor relations arena where, more often than not, pragmatic, negotiation outcomes based on compromise have prevailed over officially espoused ideologies. There is increasing hope that pragmatic flexibility may be facilitated through conflict management processes in South Africa.

REFERENCES

Adam, H. (1990, February 28). *Observations on recent political developments in South Africa*. Address at the Graduate School of Business, University of Cape Town.

Anstey, M. (1991). *Negotiating conflict*. Whetton, S.A.: Juta.

Binnedell, N. (1990). Corporate strategy and organization in the transition to democracy. *IPM Journal, 8* (12), 4–6.

Bluen, S. (1986). Industrial relations: Approaches and ideologies. In J. Barling, C. Fullagar, & S. Bluen (Eds.), *Behavior in organizations* (pp. 673–705). Johannesburg: McGraw-Hill.

Bluen, S., & Fullagar, C. (1986). Psychology and industrial relations. In J. Barling, C. Fullagar, & S. Bluen (Eds.), *Behavior in organizations* (pp. 619–670). Johannesburg: McGraw-Hill.

Blunt, P. (1985). *Organizational theory and behavior: An African perspective*. London: Longman.

Dostal, E., & Osler, K. (1990). Organization renewal. *IPM Journal, 8* (12), 17–19.

Emdin, R. (1990). The role of the industrial relations manager. *Industrial Relations Resource Document Series, 9*, 65–67.

Fisher, R., & Ury, W. (1981). *Getting to yes: Negotiating agreement without giving in*. London: Arrow Books.

Foster, D. (1986). Power, organizations and South Africa. In J. Barling, C. Fullagar, & S. Bluen (Eds.), *Behavior in organizations* (pp. 35–63). Johannesburg: McGraw-Hill.

Giliomee, H. (1990). The challenges of industrial relations in the 1990s. *Industrial Relations Journal of South Africa, 1* (2), 59–64.

Gordon, R. J. (1977). *Mines, masters and migrants*. Johannesburg: Ravan.

Greiner, L., & Schein, V. (1988). *Power and organization development*. Reading, MA: Addison-Wesley.

Hofstede, G. (1980). Motivation, leadership and organization: Do American theories apply abroad? *Organizational Dynamics, 9* (1), 42–63.

Horwitz, F. M. (1990). Human resource management: An ideological perspective. *Personnel Review, 10* (2), 12–14.

Human, L., & Icely, N. (1987). Trends in the attitudes of white workers to the upward mobility of blacks. *South African Journal of Labour Relations, 2* (1), 2.

Human, L., & Pringle, H. (1986). The attitudes of white workers to the vertical mobility of blacks. *South African Journal of Labour Relations, 10*, 304.

Human, P., & Horwitz, F. (1992). *On the edge: Managing change in South African organizations*, Kenwyn: Juta.

Jubber, K. (Ed.) (1979). *Industrial relations and industrial sociology: South Africa*. Cape Town: Juta.

Kanter, R. M. (1977). *Men and women of the corporation,* New York: Basic Books.

Keenen, J. (1984). *The B and S closure: Rationalization or reprisal.* Paper presented at the conference on economic development and racial domination, University of the Western Cape.

Kipnis, D. (1976). *The powerholders.* Chicago: University of Chicago Press.

Maller, J. (1988). ESOPS fables. Johannesburg: Labour and Economic Research Centre.

McClelland, D. C., & Boyatziz, R. E. (1982). Leadership motive matters and long-term success in management. *Journal of Applied Psychology, 67,* 737–743.

Moodie, T. D. (1980). The formal and informal social structure of a South African gold mine. *Human Relations, 33,* 555–574.

Nupen, C., & Steadman, F. (1989). Third party intervention. *Human Resource Management, 2,* 9–21.

Rahim, A. (1990, June). *A normative theory of conflict management.* Paper presented at the Third Annual Conference of the International Association for Conflict Management, Vancouver, Canada.

Savage, M. (1987). An anatomy of the South African corporate economy. *Industrial Relations Journal of South Africa, 7,* 2.

Senge, P., & Kiefer, P. (1984). Quoted in E. Dostal & K. Osler (1990). Organization renewal. *IPM Journal, 8* (12), 17–19.

Simkins, C. (1989, May). Quoted in P. de Vos. Toward one nation. *Democracy in Action, 30,* 30–35.

Strümpfer, D. (1986). Executive stress. In J. Barling, C. Fullagar & S. Bluen (Eds.), *Behavior in organizations* (pp. 535–562). Johannesburg: McGraw-Hill.

Tjosvold D. (1981). Unequal power relationships within a co-operative or competitive context. *Journal of Applied Psychology, 11,* 137–150.

Van der Merwe, H. W. (1988). A groundwork for political negotiations. *Communicare, 7,* 5–7.

———. (1989). *Pursuing justice and peace in South Africa.* London: Routledge.

Van der Merwe, H. W., Maree, J., Zaaiman, A., Philip, C., & Muller, D. (1988, December). *Principles of communication between adversaries in South Africa.* Paper presented to the International Sociological Association, Amsterdam.

Van der Merwe, H. W., & Odendaal, A. (1990, July). *Mediating for a post-apartheid South Africa.* Paper presented at the Twenty-Fifth Anniversary Conference of the International Peace Research Association, Groningen, Netherlands.

Zaleznik, A. (1990). *The managerial mystique.* New York: Harper & Row.

7

SPAIN

Lourdes Munduate, Juan Ganaza, Manuel Alcaide, and José M. Peiró

In order to fully understand conflict management in Spain, one must contextualize this phenomenon in the cultural, political, and economic environments in which it has developed. At a macro level, conflict management has played an important role in the political transition from dictatorship to democracy and European Community (EC) membership. Traditional managerial styles were inefficient for a competitive management in the frame of the Common Market. New opportunities required changes in executive potential. This entailed development in managerial styles, from traditional and autocratic management to a new conception of management, centered on dialogue, agreement, conflict resolution, and the use of procedures that imply participation. This process of adaptation of managerial attitudes and practices to the new circumstances, originated over the past few years, has brought about a series of changes in interpersonal relations and the ways or styles in which executives have assumed conflict-management at work.

A relevant characteristic of Spanish executives is that they tend to use integrating style most frequently, followed by compromising, and avoiding style least of all. A possible historical and cultural explanation for these results could be found in a certain dominance of the ideas of cooperation and integration in present Spanish society, which is somewhat related to the dominant values in Western democracies, based on the need for cooperation, dialogue, and mutual agreement among different parties in order to arrive at better solutions to problems. The rare use of alternative dispute management procedures, such as mediation, arbitration, and conciliation, is another characteristic that distinguishes Spanish from other transcultural situations. This is probably because these forms of intervention were seldom used by the official union under Franco's regime. When they were used, they clearly favored employers. Distrust toward these forms of intervention, and the common use of the judicial system, have allowed a great specialization and effectiveness of its interventions in the management of conflicts.

Spain has evolved from a rigid society, with organizations managed in an authoritarian style, as befitted a dictatorial regime, to a more tolerant, creative, and innovative society. Although this has not been an easy process, it has produced an innovative and open style that shows great respect for coexistence and diversity. Creative ways of cooperating within this diversity have appeared. Following this period of constant change, Spain presents itself as a country with a great future, thanks to its innovative flexibility and its youthful impetus. From a cultural point of view, Spanish society is oriented and situated within the Western Europe of the 1990s. Orizo's (1991) research shows that various groups coexist within this society. It points out that 40 percent of Spaniards are reluctant to work (antiwork), 40 percent accept it with a Protestant work ethic (prowork), and 20 percent value work positively but wish to make it compatible with other ways of expression in their private lives (postindustrial conception).

These values and this culture have marked the way in which organizations are managed and run and conflict is resolved within them. In this chapter we examine first the cultural, political, and social context surrounding conflict management in Spanish organizations, thus allowing the reader a more precise comprehension of its development. Later, the analysis of management styles provides a view of the most usual manners in which Spanish executives handle conflict. Third, different styles of handling interpersonal conflict management in Spanish organizations are reviewed following Rahim and Bonoma's model (1979). The main alternative dispute management procedures in Spain will be looked into, and various suggestions to improve executives' practice and research in this field will be offered.

ECONOMIC, SOCIAL, AND CULTURAL FACTORS

In order to understand the tradition of conflict management in Spain, it is necessary to look into some of the peculiarities of the cultural, political, social, and economic context in which it is carried out. The analysis of this phenomenon must consider Spanish social and political circumstances from the Spanish Civil War to the present day. It was not until democracy was established and the Constitution (1978) approved that the freedom of negotiations between unions and companies and the right to carry out industrial action in organizations were accepted.

Economic, social, and cultural factors influencing conflict-management patterns in Spain can be placed between tensions that arose from this recent past, characterized by the development of a democratic system through a political transition from a dictatorship. The immediate future is marked mostly by European Community membership and the beginning of a new political, social, and economic situation in which the nation must attempt to respond to demands of a European common currency as from 1997. The new context will be a European context, without borders or tariffs. There are great expectations in this line, resulting from the implications of a real European market, produced by the fusion of twelve national markets into one great common market of 320 million consumers (Alcaide, 1991; Peiró & Munduate, 1994).

Two aspects are especially relevant in situating the development of conflict management styles in Spain in recent years: recent political, social, cultural, and economic development, and European Community membership.

Spanish society has undergone rapid and constant transformation since 1975. It has passed in these years from an authoritarian society, in which political rights and democratic institutions were not recognized, to an open, democratic, and flexible one. All this happened in the context of an evident economic crisis, and a productive system in need of a mighty industrial reconversion and progressive modernization. This period was also characterized by a high rate of unemployment and, especially in the political transition years, a high level of labor and social conflict. Industrial relations evolved from a situation in which class unions were not legally accepted (although in these years of class struggle their influence was evident and even considerably aggressive) to a system based on free unions, even though it may have maintained certain forms of nonunion workers' representation. Collective bargaining became an integrated and accepted event. The third element of importance is the existence throughout nearly all these years (1977–84) of social pacts or agreements among unions, employers, and government that have allowed the country to overcome the difficulties of the political transition, helping to consolidate the new Spanish democracy. This third procedure developed in Spain in order to avoid labor and social conflict at a delicate moment in transition. It will be considered as an alternative dispute management procedure and will be analyzed later in the chapter. We will now concentrate on economic development and labor relations.

Two phases can be differentiated in economic development over the past ten years: a depression phase (1975–85) and an expansion phase (1985–90). The first phase is related to the 1973 international economic crisis, caused by the "oil shock." Its effect was felt especially in certain countries, such as Spain, that were not able to avoid its great impact on their unemployment rates. Spanish economy entered the 1980s with serious maladjustments caused by the events and attitudes of preceding years. Although we cannot enter into a detailed account of what occurred in Spanish society during this period, we can highlight some of the most relevant characteristics: (1) the already mentioned influence of the international economic crisis; (2) the development and consolidation of trade unions after the end of the dictatorship, which brought about union pressure to demand higher wages, improvement in labor conditions, and participation in labor and social life; (3) passivity or weakness of the transition government in facing the crisis or union pressure, due to other priorities in fundamental political and social changes taking place in the country; (4) growing loss of jobs caused by a worldwide economic crisis and an increase in job demand by youngsters and women entering the labor market.

Once political stability was reached and difficulties of the political transition were overcome in the 1980s, the basic characteristic of economic policy was the introduction of flexibility in the labor market, with the intention of ending a ten-year trend of job loss. Central government plans aimed at creating a favorable environment for profit and investment in the private sector, in order to make employment growth possible. The hypothesis was that today's profit is tomorrow's investment. Entry into the European Community at the beginning of the decade confirmed this political tendency of trust in the ability of the private sector to drive economic growth and overcome basic maladjustments in Spanish economy.

However, during the second half of the 1980s, social conflict grew due to the clash between expectations created by two successive Socialist administrations (winners of the 1982 elections) and the economic cuts. Distance between government and unions increased, leading to a general strike on December 14, 1988.

The economic policy plan involved substantial changes in the Spanish economy, mainly after 1985, despite a new rise in inflation at the end of the decade. Although the need to monitor economic growth still exists, the inflationary gap has been reduced 5.5 percent in the year in which Spain attained EC membership, to 2.5 percent five years later. The gross national product percentage increase indicates that, while Europe has grown less than 2 percent in the 1980s, Spain, even taking into consideration the first depression period, has reached 2.23 percent. This means the ultimate objective of economic policy is being reached (Alcaide, 1991; Informe Económico Financiero de Andalucía, 1989, 1990, 1991).

Another aspect that influences conflict-management patterns in Spain is evolution of labor relations from a depression phase to expansion, from 1985 onward, once democracy was consolidated and a strong Socialist government was capable of paying attention to and directing the rehabilitation policy for which the process of European convergence was calling.

The main characteristic of labor relations during the political transition is the considerable level of labor and social conflicts. There is a substantial increase in labor conflicts from 1976 to 1979, descending progressively with the social pact policy. In 1982, after forty years of dictatorship, and a period of five to seven years of transition full of doubts and fears about continuity of democracy, the Socialist party won the elections. Euphoria over this event produced a considerable decrease in labor conflicts. However, conflicts began to increase again after 1982, mainly as a result of the clash between unions' expectations about the new government, on the one hand, and increase in unemployment and flexibility in hiring regulations, on the other. This process was cushioned by pact policy among social parties. The last of these pacts, the Social and Economic Agreement (AES), signed in 1984, laid out wage progression for the following two years, and high labor conflicts of 1984, a result of the lack of social and economic agreement, were corrected. As Cádiz (1984) stated, had AES not been signed, wage rises would probably have been the same but with more conflicts and tension. After AES, increasing separation between government and unions led to a general strike in 1988. This was followed by a certain calm favored by continuity of the expansion phase and a positive evolution of the labor market. However, the Convergence Plan approved by the government in April 1992, with the intention of dealing with economic and monetary union with Europe in 1997, has been negatively valued by the unions. Its objectives imply a strict tightening of Spanish economy, and will entail drastic salary cuts and other measures, such as the reduction in unemployment benefits for agricultural workers.

A fact that merits mentioning in this brief social and economic contextualization of conflict management, due to its peculiarity, is the development of a group of industrial cooperatives, economically prosperous and democratically organized and managed in Mondragón (Basque country) during the dictatorship. These companies have been subject to many studies (Bradley & Geilb, 1981, 1983; Industrial Cooperative Association, 1985) especially from industrial sociology approaches and analyses of worker's participation in the organization of production (Greenwood & Gonzalez, 1989). What has come to be known as the Mondragón Cooperative Experience was founded in the late 1950s, once the worst moments of the economic collapse that followed Civil War and World War II had passed. Its members wished to move away from the dominating managerial context of the moment and develop a form of democratically organized company with principles based on the ideals of dignity at work and solidarity. Today, the cooperative complex of Mondragón is highly profitable, with activities as diverse as industry, housing, agriculture and food production, services, teaching, banking, and distribution, and the number of associate workers is about 22,000 (Greenwood & Gonzalez, 1989). Thomas and Logan (1980) consider that Mondragón is a real example of a system managed by workers. Although dissatisfaction and conflict do indeed exist in the cooperative, it appears to represent a very significant improvement over conventional firms (Bradley & Geilb, 1981, p. 220).

Data from Hofstede's transcultural research (1980, 1991), carried out between 1968 and 1972, are relevant for the analysis of the cultural context in which conflict management has occurred in Spain. He found certain tendencies that are coherent with the political and social situation we have described for those years. This evolution, due to the social and political changes, has been revealed in some other recent studies (Herranz, 1991; Pérez-Velasco, 1985; Vidal Abascal, 1991). Some of Spanish cultural elements are effectively reflected in the four factors Hofstede extracted from the data he obtained in his questionnaires: power distance, uncertainty avoidance, individualism, and masculinity.

In the first place, a tendency to keep a certain distance in power, together with a considerable dependence of subordinates on bosses, was characteristic of Spanish society at the beginning of the 1970s, according to Hofstede's study. This fits with the paternalistic and authoritarian way of managing organizations in Meliá and Pieró's research (1985), which showed that executives' power was mostly exercised using legitimate and reward and punishment power. Both of these are related to hierarchical structure in organizations. Haire, Ghiselli, and Porter's (1963) transcultural study about cognitive patterns in the role of the manager also points in this same direction. They situated in the same cluster Latin European countries—Spain, France, Belgium, and Italy—which tended to move together in a tight group in relation to directing, persuasion, and cooperation functions. However, Spain stood out from all others on the function of reprimanding. This function is more important, better, and more difficult in the perception of Spanish managers, and it is the least important (of these four) in the managers' repertory in other countries. This is a managerial style in which Spanish executives try to direct, cooperate, and persuade but do not hesitate to resort to threats and punishments—when the other methods fail—in order to highlight the power distance within the organization. Porat (1969) carried out a study on the effects of cultural differences on bargaining behavior in management-union conflict situations. Spanish executives failed to achieve a rapid agreement through assertive tactics more easily and rapidly than managers from other countries such as Denmark, Switzerland, or the United Kingdom. When this happened, they tended to accentuate differences with the opposing party and adopted hard and rigid tactics that make both sides lose.

In the second place, this tendency to highlight power distances is in line with the high scores Spanish executives obtained on Hofstede's (1980, 1991) uncertainty avoidance dimension. It is one of the countries ranked at the extreme of the dimension. This discomfort toward uncertainty and ambiguity is evident in the formal rules or implicit social codes with which organizations tend to regulate the behavior of their members, which reflect the psychological need for order and clarity. This management style, which emphasizes standard procedures, organizational formal structures, direct confrontation of conflict, and expression and discussion of feelings, was characteristic of the Spanish culture of the time. As García-Echevarría

(1977) points out, the executives of the 1970s tended to solve mostly administrative problems and centered on quantitative growth of the company. They postponed transition toward more qualitative aspects, such as greater transparency in management, demands of more information, more employee participation, and greater capacity and competitiveness in assuming risks. The Spanish manager of the 1980s emerged from a firm bureaucratic structure, with little capacity to assume risks and a great resistance to organizational change (García-Echevarría, 1991).

Third, the Spanish tendency toward individualism and scarce interdependence among people—as Ortega y Gasset already pointed out in 1921 in his "España invertebrada" [Nonvertebrate Spain]—together with the manifest will to maintain the aforementioned great power distance, is common to the other countries of Latin Europe. Hofstede (1980) points out that these nations are characterized by the fact that they "have a need for strict authority of hierarchical superiors, but at the same time stress their personal independence from any collectivity: They are dependent individualists" (p. 157). In this culture pattern of dependent individualism, rigid, centralized, and authoritarian social systems, in which members feel secure, are admitted. However, the direct dependence relationship, which could imply a personal involvement in work, tends to be eliminated.

The fourth factor—the feminine tendency that appears in Spanish society—reveals the fact that it is a society in which matriarchy has been extremely relevant. The role played by the mother as a central figure in the family has granted the satisfaction at work component a greater relevance than the protestant ethic and achievement components. This is in line with the avoidance of uncertainty and unknown situations that imply risks, although they may increase effectiveness. It must also be considered that, as Racionero (1985) and Filella (1987) have pointed out, many Spaniards feel that Mediterraneans have kept their capacity to enjoy life and are willing to grant that people in the United States, Britain, and Northern Europe have developed the skill of negotiating with reality through the use of high technology. This belief has led them to consider that there is very little to be learned in Spain about quality of life and a lot still to be known about technology. Spain is thus a society in which the need for affiliation, satisfaction, and good life have predominated, distancing it from an aggressive or achievement style of work, with some exceptions, such as the economically prosperous period of the American discovery (1492–1619), which coincided with an intense need of achievement in Spain (McClelland, 1961).

The features that characterized Spanish cultural context in the 1970s were comprehensible within the political and social context of the time. They can be linked to another series of dimensions considered in Hofstede's studies (1980, 1991), such as the religious (in which the high avoidance of uncertainty is shared, except in a few cases, by the Roman Catholic countries) and the linguistic (in which the Romance-language-speaking countries score medium to high on the power distance scale). Hofstede also carried out a stepwise multiple regression analysis, combining different social and economic data from the 1970s, such as the country's geographic latitude, its population size, and its economic wealth. In this analysis, Spain's position on the power distance dimension is predicted with moderate precision.

Many of the cultural values previously considered have changed with the political and social developments. Hofstede (1991) himself points this out when he analyzes the characteristics of the political system in which some of his dimensions, such as power distance, have developed: "Some elements of both extremes (large power distance–small power distance) can be found in many countries. A country like Spain, ruled dictatorially until the 1970's, has shifted remarkably smoothly to a pluralist government system" (p. 39). This political and cultural evolution has, in fact, modified the way organizations are managed and structured and how conflict is handled within them. Although not without certain resistance due the loss of relative status and changes in power relations, new methods of organizing work, such as job enrichment or semiautonomous groups and innovations for organizational change and development, have been progressively introduced (Herranz, 1991). In turn, this has led to a new value system among employees and managers. Pérez-Velasco's (1985) research about professional value hierarchies among intermediate executives shows that they feel a preference for efficacy, the contribution of professional knowledge, participation in decisions, and integration in stable work teams. At the same time, they disagree with respect to hierarchy, implication in collective actions, and the contribution of purely physical energy at work. Executives' use of procedures that imply participation (Vidal Abascal, 1991) is in agreement with these values and with Munduate, Ganaza, and Alcaide's data (1993), which show a shift toward more integrating and compromising styles in conflict management. This last study will be analyzed in detail later in the chapter.

This brief overview of Spanish political, social, economic, and cultural development over the past 25 years has shown that its society has gradually changed its values from relative intolerance, due to the need for order and clarity, to greater tolerance and capacity to absorb uncertainty; from the defense of eternal values to the search for feasible methods; from paralysis to creativity and capacity to innovate. Spanish society is now distanced from the idea the dictatorship kept alive for forty years that "Spain is different." The present attitude is closer to some ideals dealing with Europeism of the so-called 1927 generations and Ortega y Gasset's (1983) formula of 1910: "Spain is the problem, Europe is the solution" (p. 521). However, the difficulties and demands of rapid transformation haven't only involved problems. They also posed an opportunity to create a new cultural value system that would allow survival in difficult situations.

The influence of political, cultural, social, and economic factors on conflict management and negotiation in Spanish organizations can now be better understood. The interest of social scientists in this process has been reflected in the development of conflict and negotiation as a topic of study. The fact that fourteen papers at the First National Congress of Work and Organizational Psychology (in 1985) dealt with conflict management in organizations reflects this new situation. A review of the work presented in the Congress on this topic (Fernández-Ríos, 1985; Peiró & Munduate, 1994) points out various facts: (1) conflict studies have begun to emerge from obscurity; (2) organizations no longer consider conflict a nonfunctional aspect that should be avoided; (3) conflict begins to be understood as a natural phenomenon with both positive and negative consequences for the different parts of an organization. We can therefore view the late 1970s and 1980s as the beginning of studies and reviews on conflict as a functional aspect of organizations.

This period has been characterized by the proliferation of research on this subject, increasing interest in reviewing and synthesizing the main models and ideas forwarded in the United States and West European countries, and a great diversity in the orientations followed by the empirical studies. Some of the most outstanding are those carried out on conflict in organizations from a macrostructural point of view: Casado and Pérez Yruela (1975), Quijano de Arana (1982) and Fernández-Ríos (1983, 1985), who found five factors—general, psychological reactivity, environmental, relative to sanctions, and relative to trade union dynamics—as immediate causes of the development of latent conflict into manifest conflict. Munduate (1987a, 1987b, 1992), Cádiz (1984), Alcaide (1987), and Serrano (1987a, 1987b, 1988) focus on negotiation as a form of conflict management in organizations, underlining the most relevant strategies and tactics.

From a social cognitive perspective, the importance of power perception (Munduate, 1988; Munduate & Barón, 1990) and of cognitive processes (Serrano, 1990) have been analyzed. A synthesis of experimental paradigms used in negotiation processes was carried out by Martín-Domingo (1985) (see also Rodríguez, 1990).

Spain becoming a member of the European Community and consequences from this, among which the establishment of a common market with other countries is the most outstanding, marks the beginning of a new political, social, and economic situation, expressed in the European Common Act. The measures it contemplates

will produce important changes in Spanish working and business environment. On one hand, it entails the opening of new markets, access to new financial sources, possibilities for technological improvement and greater opportunities for selection of human resources, cooperation with other companies, etc. But, on the other, it also represents a series of risks and threats. It is going to imply greater competition, less protectionism, the need for more efficient management, greater challenges for product innovation and for the quality of products and services, and will require the capacity to react quickly in order to make the best of favourable opportunities and to counteract unfavourable situations (Peiró & Munduate, 1994).

Attempts already mentioned to accommodate the Spanish economy to this new European context are not far from the efforts of Spanish companies to open more to this new market. The need for Spanish corporations and companies to readjust to it are perceived as one of the main consequences of Spanish European Community membership (García-Echevarría, 1991). A survey conducted by Vidal Abascal (1991), about implications for companies of the Spanish incorporation into the EC, indicates that executives' opinions are that Spanish companies' capacity to compete has improved when they have opened to European markets. Among the factors that determine the companies' success abroad are the quality of products and services, a market position that is clear and differentiated from competitors, competitive prices, a good brand, and corporation images. Also, it seems that fields in which companies should concentrate most in the years ahead are research, development, environment, productivity, communication, and marketing. Boada, Cura, and Márquez's study (1990) shows this same tendency among executives' and specialized technicians' demands, also including quality control as a specifically mentioned field.

On the other hand, a substantial change in size and organization of companies is required. Two reasons account for this: the need to be competitive in the European context, and the development of executive potential for the training of a euromanager. Organizational change must center on the criterion of being competitive. This must be understood as the need for superior quality than that produced by the other institutions that compete within the European market. This capacity is attained by controlling the following aspects (García-Echevarría, 1991): substantial improvement in unit costs, prediction of new immediate contexts that will provide an advantageous position on the unit costs curve, and adaption strategies for new environments.

A key element in the success of this process of organizational change is the cultural change in Spanish companies through the development of new executive capacities. Until very recently they were characteristically centered on a closed national market and, therefore, had very low competitive environment conditions. As Vidal Abascal's (1991) survey shows, these organizations are conscious of this situation and tend toward a "euronational" training, with professional profiles characterized by the suppression of linguistic and cultural barriers, a broader vision of the future, and flexibility to adapt to new environments.

MANAGERIAL STYLES

Evolution in Spanish companies over the past years is possibly most noticeable in executives' profiles. As García-Echevarría (1991) points out, the Spanish managerial challenge is the executive challenge. It is the Spanish managers who have to assume the definition of the most adequate strategy to orient the company's activity toward markets and products. At the same time, they must define the most appropriate instruments for the new managerial dimension favored by the EC, by improving cooperation with foreign companies, carrying out mergers in its field, or enlarging it.

Before reflecting upon the way in which diverse managerial styles can influence conflict management styles in Spain, we must, once again, analyze their historical evolution. From a time when managers used a style that could be defined as classic, centered on hierarchy, formalist, and paternalistic, we have turned to a new way of conceiving management, centered on dialogue, agreement, conflict management, and the use of procedures that imply participation (Papeles de Economía Española, 1989; Vidal Abascal, 1991).

The first style—which we have named classic, predominant during the 1970s and has not yet disappeared—is characterized by the consideration of conflict as negative and damaging to the company. Also, managers using this style face conflict attempting to eliminate it by force, and thus becoming repressors of the situation and of their subordinates. They are managers who preferably make use of formal power (Meliá & Peiró, 1985) and therefore impose their own criteria and points of view (Papeles de Economía Española, 1989). Results of a study carried out by Porat (1969), analyzing the influence of cultural differences in the way executives of various countries handle conflict, indicated that when Spanish executives reached agreements in the early 1970s, they did so in shorter times than Danes, Swiss, or British, but the process was stopped or interrupted more often. This study concluded that Spanish executives tended to lead negotiation to a zero-sum situation in which both parties lost when they could not reach an agreement in a short time. This confirmed their lack of negotiating ability at the time. When they found themselves in confrontation situations, instead of moving conflicts toward synergy and finding common points between both parties, they adopted hard, inflexible, and highly coercive tactics. This tended to provoke greater antagonism among parties and unleashed a spiral of vindictive and coercive actions, creating an impasse very difficult to resolve.

As García-Echevarría (1991) pointed out, in relation to national classic indicators of executives' characteristics, Spanish executives emerge from a structure strongly linked to bureaucratic organizational schemes, with a relatively low weight of leadership capacity and risk assumption and conflict management. This characteristic of Spanish executives, present even in the first years of the 1980s, is considered by some authors (Boada, Cura, & Márquez, 1990, p. 234)

> as a continuity of styles and methods that were useful in the eco-
> nomic adventure of the seventies, and, consequently, they were not
> capable of understanding the implications of the future long crisis.
> The consolidation of democracy did not solve the economic situation
> in the first half of the decade . . . [and] the impending mentality was
> to resist at whatever cost.

Therefore, there is an interpretation that shows the very little participatory and democratic management style predominating among Spanish executives in the 1960s and 1970s. However, other studies have pointed out that this might not be the element that differentiates Spanish managerial culture from others. Data of some cross-cultural research about similarities and differences in managers' attitudes among different countries sustain this hypothesis. The study carried out by Haire, Ghiselli, and Porter (1963) about cultural patterns in the role of manager included eleven different countries, such as the United States, Spain, and Denmark, and arrived at two conclusions relevant to our discussion. First, no great differences among attitudes and managerial practices of executives of different nationalities were found. "At least in their expressed conviction, however, [the national managerial stereotypes] do not appear sharply. Managers views on how to manage people are somewhat similar [among countries]" (p. 301). In the second place, although the ideas about managerial practice have been persuasive and participatory, the basic conviction about the nature of people remains rather traditional and unchanged. The authors point out that this paradox between a lack of basic confidence in others and at the same time a leaning toward participative, group-centered cooperation could be the effect of the partial acceptance of modern management concepts.

In any case, Haire et al. (1963) do present some differences worth mentioning. They distinguish among four nationality groups, with similar oscillations within each one: the Anglo-Saxon pair (England and the United States); Japan isolated from the rest; the four continental European countries with a strong Latin background (France, Spain, Belgium, and Italy), which move together rather tightly and can probably be usefully distinguished from the Northern European/Scandinavian group (Germany, Norway, Sweden, and Denmark). Due to the ethnic affinity of these clusters, the authors conclude that the patterns of management beliefs about superior-subordinate relationships are practically explicable in terms of cultural traditions in the countries. "Management beliefs seem shaped more by [cultural] traditions than by degree or kind of industrialization. . . . France, Spain, Belgium and Italy, a diverse package as far as industrialization is concerned, tend to swing together" (p. 303). These last results coincide with Alexander, Barrett, Bass, and Ryterband's data (1971), in a comparative study among seven countries, that show the skill to empathize displayed by people with a Latin background. Hofstede's transcultural data (1980, 1991) show that Latin European countries adopt similar positions on individualism and power distance dimensions. The Latin European cluster—in which France, Belgium, Italy, and Spain are situated and into which South Africa is entering—tend to maintain a medium high power distance and a scarce mutual interdependence.

It seems, according to this data, that the classic profile of the Spanish executive can be shared by a large body of managers in each country, at least in what is referred to basic conceptions about people's capacities of implication and initiative. On the other hand, orientation toward people, empathy skills, and tendency to maintain good interpersonal relations is common to certain European countries of Latin influence, although some national differences do exist. As Filella (1987) has observed more recently in his work on management development in Spain, despite the stereotypical Spanish executive, some training programs carried out in Spanish companies, such as Bimbo, Vulca, and La Caixa, follow the same pattern as other European programs oriented to help people learn and grow personally. Also, recent studies about strategies and tactics employed by different parties in collective bargaining negotiations, and roles adopted by both union and management representatives, indicate a current trend to display confrontation in a more open fashion, with more assertive and less authoritarian techniques being employed by management in conflict situations. Thus, in the analysis of negotiation, Serrano and Remeseiro (1987) found significant differences in attitudes toward the other party among union representatives and management. Unions showed a more negative attitude toward their opponents than managers. Likewise, Remeseiro and Méndez (1988) found that persuasive tactics were employed mostly by management, whereas coercive procedures were used only by the unions, who combined them with persuasive tactics.

Returning to present use of managerial styles, it can be observed that the values and attitudes of the Spanish manager have changed considerably over the last few years. Vidal Abascal (1991, p. 18) notes that

> the figure of the leading manager that controls all the productive process has evolved to an executive that is part of a great corporation ... and that must be in a position to make the organization attractive. The new manager must question his value hierarchy, and place values such as long-term vision and managerial communication above profitability or economic factors.

Results of Vidal Abascal's study on the profile of the executives of the 1990s do indicate a change in traditional conception of company managers' activities. Among outstanding qualities are the following, in order of importance: (1) long-term vision, (2) flexibility to respond to a changing environment, (3) knowing how to motivate work teams and foster individual capabilities, (4) knowledge of how to run the company according to local customs without losing the overall view of the organization, and (5) capability in maintaining fluent relations in various languages.

In multinational companies flexibility to respond to a changing environment is placed above long-term vision. These results coincide with tendencies shown in the euromanager's definition profile (García-Echevarría, 1991). It is expected that the European managers of the next years will have, in first place, a greater long-term vision, meaning the capability to perceive adequately the best product/market opportunities that will allow the development of their corporations' possibilities. In the second place, a greater ability to work in teams is expected, as well as the competence to assume autonomous management of business or organizational units under their responsibility. In other words, what is required is the generation of management styles that reduce costs of resistance to change (García-Echevarría, 1991).

STYLES OF HANDLING INTERPERSONAL CONFLICT

The analysis of management style on a micro level, in a way that permits the comprehension of how individual managers handle conflict with their superiors, subordinates, and peers, is useful to understand conflict-handling styles in the Spanish cultural context. We have already pointed out that until recently the Spanish political situation has not favored the study of conflict and its resolution, so available data are rather scarce.

Munduate, Ganaza, and Alcaide (1993) have recently analyzed the use of the different conflict-management or -handling styles among Spanish managers, and verify whether there are important differences between these behavior patterns and those obtained in other investigations carried out in different cultural situations. The instrument used to assess the behavior of subjects in conflict situations was the Rahim Organizational Conflict Inventory–II (ROCI–II) (Rahim, 1983a), based on a two-dimensional approach: attempt to satisfy one's own concerns and attempt to satisfy the concerns of the other person. A combination of the dimensions results in five different handling conflict styles: integrating, obliging, dominating, avoiding, and compromising. The questionnaire had three different forms, A, B and C, which differed only in whether conflict relations were considered with a superior, a peer, or a subordinate. The demographic variables considered were sex, educational level, organizational status, functional area, and role played by the other actor or party.

The sample was 226 subjects, 193 men and 30 women, with a mean age of forty. All subjects in the sample were carrying out tasks of executive nature, and represented top (N = 47), middle (N = 142), and lower (N = 36) executive levels, and belonged to six functional areas. The translated and adapted ROCI–II obtained a Cronbach alpha of .78 for the total scale. Reliability estimates of the five scales of conflict styles of the adapted instrument were the following: integrating, alpha = .77; obliging, alpha= .76; dominating, alpha = .75; avoiding, alpha = .70; and compromising, alpha = .62. The factor analysis showed that the five different conflict management styles structure is valid in Spanish cultural context. Table 7.1 shows the differences obtained in the five styles as a function of referent role, organizational level, functional area, and education. Comments on the five interpersonal conflict management styles, as studied by Munduate, Ganaza, and Alcaide (1993) are included in the following paragraphs.

Integrating

It can be said that this is the dominating style among Spanish executives. Results seem to indicate that over the past years there has been a shift in organizations and among their members from paternalistic behaviors to attitudes more prone to dialogue, open treatment of problems, search for common agreements, and cooperation.

We believe this evolution is very much related to the events and behavior patterns adopted during the democratic transition period (since the mid-1970s). The most outstanding values at that moment were dialogue, social peace, agreement, and search for solutions that responded to common interests. This tendency to avoid confrontation and managers' use of more assertive and less authoritarian techniques is specially evident in Serrano and Remeseiro's work (1987) . Vidal Abascal's (1991) and Osorio's (1992) studies confirmed a future tendency to use the integrating style. They observed that procedures that imply participation, flexibility, a disposition to learn, and the ability to conduct work teams were the aspects most valued by Spanish managers, when they were asked to consider the profile of the euromanager of the 1990s. The results that appear in Table 7.1 show that:

- Spanish executives, in general, seem to present a tendency to predominantly use the integrating style.
- The organizational level does not involve significant differences in the frequencies of the use of this style.
- It seems that marketing executives present a greater tendency to use this style than executives from other functional areas. This could be explained by the fact that the members of marketing departments are in a position in which they have to find a compromise between the company's interests and those of the customer. They would, therefore, develop a greater sensibility toward other people's interests.

Table 7.1
Managerial Reference Group Norms of Style of Handling Interpersonal Conflict (Spain) (N = 226)

Variable	N	Integrating			Obliging			Dominating			Avoiding			Compromising		
		M	SD	F	M	SD	F	M	SD	F	M	SD	F	M	SD	F
Referent Role				2.46*			15.10*			3.47*			0.96			3.69*
Superior	77	4.26	.51		3.44	.71		3.09	.69		3.30	.72		3.78	.57	
Subordinates	73	4.16	.51		2.92	.51		2.96	.87		3.37	.70		3.62	.62	
Peers	76	4.34	.43		3.09	.52		2.76	.75		3.46	.71		3.88	.51	
Organizational Level				0.07			0.06			0.87			1.51			0.10
Top	47	4.25	.56		3.18	.65		3.01	.73		3.25	.77		3.79	.57	
Middle	142	4.26	.48		3.14	.64		2.88	.81		3.44	.69		3.76	.55	
Lower	36	4.28	.42		3.17	.56		3.04	.73		3.30	.67		3.74	.70	
Functional Area				2.77*			2.13*			1.07			1.61			1.56
Production	29	4.16	.46		3.14	.68		3.04	.82		3.67	.73		3.82	.56	
Marketing	16	4.60	.31		3.58	.56		3.01	.56		3.48	.76		4.03	.46	
Finance & Accounting	35	4.23	.48		3.05	.65		2.74	.77		3.33	.77		3.61	.56	
General Management	32	4.15	.52		3.17	.64		3.10	.74		3.27	.75		3.72	.65	
Other	113	4.28	.49		3.12	.59		2.91	.81		3.33	.65		3.77	.57	
Education				2.56*			2.35*			0.72			2.34*			2.13*
Estudios Primarios	9	4.49	.41		3.28	.32		3.31	.57		3.78	.74		4.03	.48	
E.G.B.	13	4.33	.39		3.17	.65		2.94	.82		3.79	.75		3.96	.64	
F.P.1.	8	4.46	.23		3.56	.62		3.13	.90		3.81	.55		4.03	.56	
B.U.P.	17	4.39	.41		3.45	.59		3.16	.95		3.37	.71		3.95	.56	
F.P.2.	20	4.21	.49		3.21	.68		2.84	.77		3.28	.66		3.65	.75	
C.O.U.	22	4.14	.49		3.26	.65		2.80	.74		3.24	.74		3.65	.38	
Titulación Media	69	4.36	.48		3.17	.60		2.90	.75		3.41	.66		3.82	.55	
Titulación Superior	66	4.09	.51		2.94	.61		2.91	.76		3.20	.67		3.60	.54	
Total sample	226	4.26	.49		3.15	.63		2.94	.79		3.38	.71		3.76	.58	

Note: N = Sample size; M = Mean; SD = Standard deviation; F = F-ratio; Education—Estudios Primarios = Certificate obtained through assistance to elementary and junior high without attaining minimum educational level, E.G.B.= Elementary and junior high, F.P.1 = Technical college (ages 14 to 15), F.P.2 = Technical college (ages 16 to 18), B.U.P. = High school, C.O.U. = Pre-university college, Titulación Media = Three year university courses, Titulación Superior = Five year university courses

*p < .05

- Although there do not appear to be significant differences in the use of the integrating style with the role played by the other party, a certain predominance of this style can be found among equals.

- Finally, it must be pointed out that the use of integration increases when the educational status of the parties decreases.

Obliging

This style consists essentially of placing other party's interests before one's own. One logically concludes that it must be one of the least popular conflict-handling styles, because it implies losing and letting the other win. However, Spaniards tend to use this style more than the dominating style. Some of the characteristics of Spanish managers in the use of this style are:

- The frequency in its use increases with the status or hierarchical level of the other party. For example, employees are more obliging toward the boss than toward equals, and more toward these than with subordinates.

- Educational status also seems to be related to the use of this style: it decreases with higher educational status.

- No great differences are observed in relation to organizational level. High-, medium-, and low-level executives show fairly similar frequencies in the use of this style. In turn, they do not differ greatly from the general average.

Dominating

In a certain way, it could be said that this has been the predominating style of Spanish executives for many years. It cannot be forgotten that until the mid-1970s democratic rights did not formally exist in Spain. However, over the years and due to the important protest movements of the 1970s, this style has started to lose importance in companies (García-Echevarría, 1991). Spanish executives' assessment of the use of an authoritarian style by euromanagers (Osorio, 1992) indicates that this tendency will become even more noticeable in the future. Data in Table 7.1 reflect this same orientation. The most relevant features of this style are:

- In practically every case this is the least frequent style among Spanish executives.

- There is a tendency to use the dominating style in the least balanced relations. For example, it is less frequent among equals than in relations with bosses or subordinates.

- There are no significant differences among hierarchical levels, functional areas, or educational status.

Avoiding

This style consists basically in giving problems time to sort themselves out. It implies not recognizing or attempting to smooth out conflict. Spanish executives' most outstanding characteristics in relation to this style are:

- It is rare among executives with higher educational status.
- Although without significant differences, it seems to be more usual among intermediate executives than among low-level executives, and more frequent among these than among the higher levels.
- No significant differences are observed either among functional areas or relative positions of rivals.

Compromising

This is the second most frequent technique among Spanish executives, although at a certain distance from the first. This is in line with the tendency, found in other studies (Serrano & Remeseiro, 1987), of avoidance of confrontation and use of assertive tactics by executives in managing conflict situations. Table 7.1 shows the most relevant features of this style:

- Compromising holds a greater presence among lower educational status executives than among higher educational status executives.
- Compromising tactics are used less with subordinates than with bosses, and less with these than with equals.
- Hierarchical level does not determine in an evident manner the frequency in which this style is used.
- Although without significant relevance, it does seem that marketing executives are, once again, the ones who make a greater use of this style.

The comparison with Rahim's (1992) sample of American executives (see Figure 7.1) shows that Spanish managers tend to use compromising, integrating, and obliging styles most. On the other hand, dominating and obliging styles have a lower ratio in the Spanish sample. However, both samples have similar profiles.

From what has been presented, it would seem that an important characteristic of Spanish managers is that they seem to have a common pattern in the relationships among integrating, compromising, and

Figure 7.1
Styles of Handling Interpersonal Conflict (Spain)

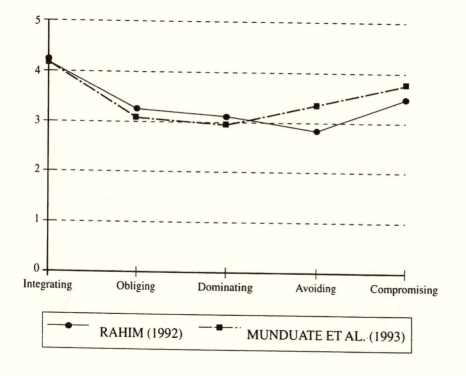

avoiding styles. Note that these three styles are situated along what has been called the integrative dimension of conflict management. Regardless of which variable is taken into consideration in Table 7.1, and in all cases, the integrating style is the most frequent, followed by compromise and, last of all, avoiding. A possible historical and cultural explanation for these results could be found in a certain dominance of the ideas of cooperation and integration in present Spanish society, as we saw earlier.

ALTERNATIVE DISPUTE MANAGEMENT

The most important mechanisms that are used in Spain in order to solve collective or individual labor conflicts (among employers and employees or their representatives) are mainly judicial. They either consist of turning to ordinary labor courts or requesting the state's direct intervention. However, apart from these judicial mechanisms, a series of alternative dispute management (ADM) techniques have been developed. In any case, these procedures are rarely used or have little relevance. The underlying reasons for this are:

1. Spanish social actors have a general lack of confidence in third parties, except for judicial authorities, when it comes to solving labor conflicts. Two reasons can explain this: the absence of them during the predemocracy years, and when these procedures did appear, they were clearly aimed at replacing the right to undertake industrial action—in other words, at avoiding strikes.

2. There are positive aspects of decisions adopted by the judicial authorities on labor matters. Courts dealing with these types of situations in Spain are highly specialized, professional, and very effective in the labor relations system.

3. Social parties clearly overvalue judicial decisions in the solution of work conflicts (Rey, 1992).

We will, however, albeit the insufficiencies and problems pointed out, comment on the most relevant characteristics of the ADM techniques employed in Spain. These techniques can be grouped under the categories of mediation, conciliation, and arbitration. The available statistical data on the subject do not show a clear distinction between conciliation and mediation interventions, although they do distinguish these two from arbitration. As a matter of fact, Rey (1992) points out that in practice the distinction between conciliation and mediation in Spain, as in other countries (Goldman, 1985), is an artificial one, especially when one is dealing with interest conflicts.

Spanish legislation does not regulate *conciliation*, but it is considered that all interventions that imply a "passivity" in the third party, in a context of total freedom of the other parties involved, are included under this denomination (Rey, 1992). If considered in this way, conciliation would be the ADM technique most used in Spain (Anuario de Estadísticas Laborales, 1990; Hernández, 1992).

Spanish regulations and legal doctrine consider mediation an active intervention of a third party without the power to take a final decision. A study that has classified the scarce mediation interventions that have occurred in Spain proposed grouping them under the following categories (Rey, 1992): political mediation, administrative mediation, ad hoc mediation, tripartite mediation, and labor inspector mediation. Political mediation takes place in the final phases of negotiation, with a political representative without any specialization in these kinds of affairs acting as mediator. It is considered an exceptional intervention and its objective is the reduction of the level of labor disputes. Administrative mediation is clearly bureaucratic. It follows rigid and formalized procedures, has no specialization, and is carried out by the official institutions belonging to the labor administration such as the General Office for Mediation, Arbitration, and Conciliation. Ad hoc mediation is of a specialized nature, without administrative inclinations—it is more flexible—and follows strictly technical and nonpolitical criteria. In tripartite mediation there are not only a mediator and the affected parties, but also other third parties such as union and management officials that manifest certain interests in the existing dispute. Although the mediator may be a specialist, he or she does not act as a professional mediator. The mediator's recommendations are presented by a joint committee (the tripartite committee) in which the "conciliating" parties also represent the interests of the "affected" parties. The last modality of mediation, carried out by the labour inspection, is specialized, nonprofessional, technical, informal, and restricted to certain cases. The scarcity of this type of intervention is because it interferes with the labor authorities' normal sanctioning role. The labor inspectors are responsible for the surveillance of the implementation of labor regulations, collective agreements, timetables, and working conditions and employees' rights.

The different *arbitration procedures* have some common features: they are not often used, they are procedures that are not very concrete nor very much structured, and their regulation is perceived as being insufficient and unsatisfactory.

Paritary committees should also be mentioned in this context. They are commitees for mediation, arbitration, and conciliation established in some collective agreements, in order to solve differences that may arise in industrial relations. However, sometimes the agreements reached in these committees are legally inefficient, because they are contradicted by the resolutions emitted by the labor authorities. This disparity is tending to be progressively reduced (Rey, 1992).

Apart from these judicial methods and the ADM techniques already described, since the early 1970s Spain has developed social pacts, which are alternative ways of managing collective disputes. Social pacts are agreements among unions, employers, and government in order to avoid labor and social conflict. These pacts have been macroeconomic conflict resolution techniques characterized by the participation of the three social agents: management, unions, and government. They have managed to prevent, channel, and solve labor conflicts harmonizing different interests in dispute. Herranz (1991, p. 182) points out that "from the middle of the 1970s, tendencies could be observed toward a greater strengthening of negotiations at the top level and the development of social agreements on the national level. These can be seen as a strategy to control the labour movement and to stabilize democracy."

After the establishment of democracy, several national-level social agreements were reached: the Moncloa Pact in 1977, the Acuerdo Marco Interfederal (AMI) in 1980, the National Agreement of Employment (ANE) in 1981, the Acuerdo Interfederal (AI) in 1984, and the Social and Economic Agreement (AES) for 1985/1986 signed in 1984. These pacts attempted to achieve various objectives, such as increasing productivity, improving working conditions, intensifying control over absenteeism, and containing unemployment. The pact from 1983, the AI, introduced salary restrictions and stimulated investment and flexible dismissal. Despite this circumstance, the agreement allowed, as others had before, a considerable reduction of labor conflicts and was possible thanks to popular and union support for the recent Socialist government. Those social pacts came to establish cooperation in place of confrontation as a means of facing the nation's precarious economic situation (Cádiz, 1984; Espina 1991).

The influence of these negotiations was reflected in two substantial aspects of the country's economy: (1) industrial conflict, except for a few exceptions, has decreased every year from 1978, falling from 171 million hours lost on strike activities in 1979 to 49 million in 1991; (2) wage rises and inflation rates were reduced in the second half of the 1980s, due to the control established on them following the signing of these agreements.

DISCUSSION

In order to fully understand conflict management in Spain, one must place this phenomenon in the cultural, political, and economic environment in which it has developed. At a macro level, conflict management has played an important role in the political transition from dictatorship to democracy and European Community membership. Until the mid-1970s, Spain lived under a Franquist regime that determined an authoritarian management style, a protected market, and a state interventionist policy toward labor relations, in which workers' most elementary rights were not recognized. In any case, and despite this authoritarian context, certain experiences in industrial democracy, such as the cooperatives of Mondragón, were possible. These attempts pointed toward the need for managerial systems that contemplated workers' participation and management. The transition from a paternalistic culture, favored by a politically authoritarian regime, to a more open, plural, free, egalitarian, individualistic, and democratic one, has been one of the most outstanding cultural factors in Spanish society influencing conflict management.

This period of transition from an autocratic society to a modern and participative one, integrated in Europe without boundaries or tariffs and sharing a common market, has been carried out during a phase of acute economic crisis, accompanied by a considerable increase in unemployment, a high level of labor and social conflict, and an important transformation of the labor market. Facing this critical situation at such a moment, and responding at the same time to competition in the European context, required a collective effort of Spanish society, stressing cooperative ties among social groups, and undertaking substantial changes in the size and management and administration of organizations. Traditional managerial styles were inefficient for a competitive management in the European Community. New opportunities for the nation required changes in executive potential. This entailed development in managerial styles, from classical unilateral directive management, to a new conception of management, centered on dialogue, agreement, conflict resolution, and the use of procedures that imply participation. We have, however, mentioned Haire, Ghiselli, and Porter's study (1963), in which the managerial style that we have named classic, predominant during the 1960s and 1970s in Spanish organizations, did not differ greatly from attitudes and practices of executives worldwide, or at least in the Latin context, at that moment. Some recent reports (García-Echevarría, 1991; Vidal Abascal, 1991) have shown an effort on the part of Spanish executives to adapt to the profile of European manager for the next years, depicted as having a greater long-term view, flexibility to respond quickly in a changing environment, greater capability for teamwork, and a command over community languages.

This process of adaptation of managerial attitudes and practices to the new circumstances, originated over the past few years, has brought about a series of changes in interpersonal relations and the ways or styles in which executives have assumed conflict management at work. Various instruments have been developed to assess the behavior of subjects in conflict situations. One of these, ROCI–II (Rahim, 1983a) is useful for the description of interpersonal conflict management in different cultural contexts (Bergman & Volkema, 1989; Lee, 1990; Rahim, 1983b, 1986; Van de

Vliert & Kabanoff, 1990; Weider-Hatfield, 1988). Data obtained by Mun-duate, Ganaza, and Alcaide (1993), using ROCI–II, show that the five dif-ferent conflict-management styles structure on which Rahim's instrument is based is valid for Spanish cultural context, and that Spanish executives tend to use different styles according to whether they interact with superi-ors (with whom they employ obliging style), subordinates (dominating and compromising style), or with peers (compromising style). Spanish ex-ecutives have higher average scores on all styles, except dominating and obliging, than their American counterparts (Rahim, 1992), although both samples show a similar profile. A relevant characteristic of Spanish execu-tives is that they tend to use integrating style most frequently, followed by compromise, and avoiding style least of all. A possible historical and cul-tural explanation for these results could be found in a certain dominance of the ideas of cooperation and integration in present Spanish society, which is somewhat related to the dominant values in Western democra-cies, based on the need for cooperation, dialogue, and mutual agreement among different parties in order to arrive at better solutions to problems.

If the transition period required an effort to increase interpersonal and intergroup cooperation in conflict management in organizations, at a more macro level it brought about a policy of pacts or agreements among social interlocutors that, rather than being a managerial policy, was aimed at the consolidation of democracy. The peculiarity of social pacts or agreements among unions, employers, and government throughout the political tran-sition period reflects the most outstanding alternative dispute manage-ment procedure in Spain. The rare use of alternative dispute management procedures, such as mediation, arbitration, and conciliation, is another characteristic that distinguishes Spanish from other transcultural situa-tions. This is probably because these other forms of intervention were not used by the Franquist vertical unions, and when they were, they clearly fa-vored employers. Distrust toward these forms of intervention, and the common use of the judicial system, have allowed a great specialization and effectiveness of its interventions in the management of conflicts.

Following this revision, we can point to some suggestions that could im-prove executive capabilities and skills in order to deal with the challenges that face the Spanish company. To confront competition in the European market, managerial strategies must (1) improve production costs through a correct coordination and distribution of resources, and (2) carry out an ad-equate selection of context, markets, and products. Also, executive training programs must be oriented basically toward covering companies' new needs favoring managerial styles that reduce the costs of adapting to new markets. In order to develop Spanish managers' potential and a broader long-term view, the constitution of working teams and flexibility to adapt to changing environments must be promoted. In this line, confronting com-petition will consist of coordinating companies' potential and new markets.

Although certain interpretations maintain a stereotype of the Spanish executive distant from the profile required for the future, other views indicate that this process of adaptation to more participating styles, in which information and objectives are shared among superiors and subordinates, with great flexibility to adapt to different situations and problems, is common to most executives in general. Rahim (1992) proposes that, in addition to this flexibility in executives' practices, organizations should take care of their level of conflict: "effectiveness can be maximized if a moderate amount of conflict is maintained and organizational members use different styles of conflict depending on situations" (p. 30). Rahim's (1985, 1992) argument centers on the need for an adequate comprehension of conflict management to contemplate both the "amounts of conflict" present in an organization and the "styles of interpersonal conflict" used by organizational participants.

Assessment of the first aspect will allow us to know the distance between level of conflict in the organization and level required for optimal effectiveness, and "by analyzing the conflict-handling styles of organizational members, researchers can obtain information about the appropriateness or effectiveness of each style for particular situations" (Weider-Hatfield, 1988, p. 351). In this sense, although in Spain various alternative procedures to maintain labor conflict levels within acceptable limits have been proposed and developed—pact policy among social parties, judicial intervention, and preventive strategies such as participatory management—improvement of interpersonal conflict management styles has not been considered to a lesser degree.

Rahim's (1983a) ROCI–II could be a useful instrument for training applications, as it already has proven its utility in other contexts (Weider-Hatfield, 1988). One of its advantages is that, being a questionnaire with three forms that differ only in reference to conflict with a boss (Form A), subordinate (Form B), or peers (Form C), it can be used in conflict-management workshops with groups composed of both managerial and nonmanagerial personnel. It is designed for easy self-administration. Although we do not yet have scales for Spanish populations, if the trainer is limited to interpreting participants' scores, the general norms provided by Rahim (1983a, 1992) from the 1,219 managers of his original sample allow a basis of comparison to determine how frequently a respondent relies on a particular style. However, though it does show members' tendency to use certain styles, these norms do not provide information as to whether or not the respondents use the styles appropriately (Weider-Hatfield, 1988).

Weider-Hatfield also points out that ROCI–II is associated with a comprehensive model for diagnosing and intervening in organizational conflict (Rahim, 1985, 1992; Rahim & Bonoma, 1979), based on the five conflict-management styles introduced by Blake and Mouton (1964, 1970).

In this sense, Rahim's model can be useful in transcultural research, for four reasons. First because, as has already been mentioned, it offers a wide range of styles of handling interpersonal conflict that has been contrasted in various cultural settings. Second, its implications suggest that it is best to know how to employ all styles, allowing Rahim's model's application to the flexibility required of future executives. Third, because it points to the need of knowing the situations most appropriate for the use of each style. And fourth, because this suggestion is complemented with available training proposals for the use of these different interpersonal conflict management styles.

Despite the vertiginous changes occurring in Spanish labor relations, from a protectionist model to another in which parties' autonomy during collective bargaining is favored, the government's role has greatly mediated labor negotiations during most of the period. By means of a three-way pact policy (government, management, and unions), cooperation among social parties has predominated over confrontation, considered wrong in view of the country's precarious economic situation (Cádiz, 1984). It is not necessary to choose between the two extremes of institutionalization of social consensus as a negotiation framework, at a moment in which there is strong pressure to substantially reduce inflation, as agreed in the EC meeting at Maastricht, and a system of strong social confrontation. Tradition of conflict management in North and Central European nations over the last years advises that, although admiring differences of interests among parties, integration strategies distant from legalistic preciseness and power tensions should be adopted. The development of third-party intervention acting with arbitration, mediation, or conciliation roles, without partisan intentions of preceding years, and linked to practices common in other countries such as the United Kingdom (Dickens, 1979) or the United States (Carnevale & Pruitt, 1992), could be useful in promoting this tendency to play conflict within cooperation.

Finally, future research could adapt prescriptions and research topics on design and management of organizations arising from the quality of work-life (QWL) approach (Mohrman, Ledford, Lawler, & Mohrman, 1986) for validity in the Spanish cultural context. We have observed that traditional design and management strategies are being seriously questioned and new ones are rapidly being introduced. As Mohrman et al. point out, "the change is motivated by necessity. Today's organizations cannot afford to organize for predictability and control in a world where adaptiveness and responsiveness are the main determinants of effectiveness and survival. Many of the new practices are ripe topics for research" (pp. 212–213). Since flexibility, long-term vision, and teamwork capacity are required in the future executives' profile, the tasks of selection, feedback, and reward must include the group level of analysis, and must begin to look more like cooperation than control. Research into these topics and others related to managerial styles and personnel management issues requires attention.

Research on conflict management styles shows that data on relations between referent role and conflict styles in Spain (Munduate, Ganaza, & Alcaide, 1993) are similar to those obtained by other authors (Rahim, 1983a, 1986, 1992). They suggest that managers are more obliging with superiors, integrating with subordinates (despite the fact that they are more dominating and compromising in Spain), and compromising with their peers.

Orientation of future research in alternative dispute management can also be guided by proposals arising from the QWL approach. "There is evidence that labor relations in our society are in a period of significant transformation in the direction of more cooperative efforts to address the mutual interests of labor and management. . . . Academic researchers working within the QWL framework have advocated cooperation between the union and company in addressing issues of mutual concern" (Mohrman et al., 1986, pp. 209–210) . Due to tradition in social pacts and judicial intervention in Spanish cultural context, it could be useful to design "experiments" that would allow us to observe what happens when parties attempt to cooperate, both under a freedom margin limited by macrosocial pacts and when no previous framework exists. The observation of results with third-party intervention (mediation, arbitration, or conciliation) could be undertaken, considering Spanish cultural features. Another field of study could be the development of preventive modes of conflict that foster QWL by involving executives. As Stephenson and Brotherton (1979) and Hartley and Kelly (1986) have pointed out, social psychology can contribute greatly, both theoretically and methodologically, to the study of cooperation in significant problem solving and the effect of third-party intervention on long-term relations between parties in conflict.

REFERENCES

Alcaide, M. (1987). *Conflicto y poder en las organizaciones* [Conflict and power in organizations]. Madrid: Centro de Publicaciones del Ministerio de Trabajo y Seguridad Social.
Alcaide, M. (1991) . El futuro del empleo en la CEE. [The future of employment in the EEC]. *Relaciones Laborales, 2*, 74–91.
Alexander, R. A., Barrett, G. K., Bass, B. M, & Ryterband, F. C. (1971). Empathy, protection, and negation in seven countries. In L. E. Abt & B. F. Riess (Eds.), *Clinical psychology in industrial organizations* (pp. 29–49). New York: Grune & Stratton.
Anuario de Estadísticas Laborales [Annals of Labor Statistics] (1990). Madrid: Ministerio de Trabajo y Seguridad Social.
Bergman, T. J., & Volkema, R. J. (1989). Understanding and managing interpersonal conflict at work: Its issues, interactive processes, and consequences. In M. A.

Rahim (Ed.) *Managing conflict: An interdisciplinary approach* (pp. 7–19). New York: Praeger.

Bradley, K., & Geilb, A. (1981). Motivation and control in the Mondragón experiment. *British Journal of Industrial Relations, 25*, 211–240.

Bradley, K., & Geilb, A. (1983). *Cooperation at work: The Mondragón experience.* London: Heineman Educational Books.

Blake, R. R., & Mouton, J. S. (1964). *The managerial grid.* Houston: Gulf.

Blake, R. R., & Mouton, J. S. (1970). The fifth achievement. *Journal of Applied Behavioral Science, 6*, 413–436.

Boada, F., Cura, J., & Márquez, J. M. (1990). 1980–1990: Una década a través de los ejecutivos españoles. [1980–1990: A decade in Spanish executives]. *Alta Dirección, 25*, 169–240.

Cádiz, A. (1984). *Conflicto y negociación* [Conflict and negotiation]. Madrid: Ibérico Europea de Ediciones.

Carnavale, P. J., & Pruitt, D. G. (1992). Negotiation and mediation. *Annual Review of Psychology, 43*, 551–582.

Casado, D., & Pérez Yruela, M. (1975). *Organización, conflicto y estrategias de negociación* [Organization, conflict and negotiation strategies] . Madrid: Hálar.

Dickens, L. (1979). Conciliation, mediation and arbitration in British Industrial Relations. In G. M. Stephenson and C. J. Brotherton (Eds), *Industrial relations: A social psychological approach* (pp. 289–307). Chichester: Wiley.

Espina, A. (1991). *Empleo, democracia y relaciones industriales en España* [Employment, democracy and industrial relations in Spain]. Madrid: Ministerio de Trabajo y Seguridad Social.

Fernández-Ríos, M. (1983). *La conflictividad laboral latente: factores psicosociales* [Latent industrial conflict: Social psychological factors]. Unpublished doctoral dissertation, Universidad Autónoma de Madrid.

Fernández-Ríos, M. (1985). Un modelo multidimensional para el análisis de situaciones conflictuales [A multidimensional model for the analysis of conflict situations]. In *Presente y futuro de la psicología del trabajo en la empresa* [Present and future of work psychology in companies] (pp. 139–144). Madrid: Fundación Universidad-Empresa.

Filella, J. C. (1987). Management development in India and Spain. In B. M. Bass & P.J.D. Drenth (Eds), *Advances in organizational psychology: An international review* (pp. 123–135). London: Sage.

García-Echevarría, S. (1977). El nuevo directivo español [The new Spanish manager]. *Alta Dirección, 13*, 101–104.

García-Echevarría, S. (1991). Dirección de la empresa y el ejecutivo del futuro [Management and the executive of the future] *Alta Dirección, 157*, 59–176

Goldman, A. (1985). Settlement of disputes over interests. In R. Blanpain (Ed.), *Comparative labour law and industrial relations* (pp. 359–387). Deventer: Kluwer.

Greenwood, D., & Gonzalez, J. L. (1989). *Culturas de fagor* [Fagor's cultures]. San Sebastián: Txertoa.

Haire, M., Ghiselli, E., & Porter, L. W. (1963). Cultural patterns in the role of the manager. *Institute of Industrial Relations, 2*, 95–117.

Hartley, J., & Kelly, J. (1986). Psychology and industrial relations: From conflict to cooperation? *Journal of Occupational Psychology, 59*, 161–176.

Hernández, J. (1992). *La solución de los conflictos en el sistema de relaciones laborales* [Conflict resolution in the labor relations system]. Madrid: Ministerio de Trabajo y Seguridad Social.

Herranz, R. (1991) . New forms of work organization. The case of Spain. In P. Gootings, B. Gustavsen, & L. Hethy (Eds.), *New forms of work organizations in Europe* (pp. 175–192). New Brunswick, NJ: Transaction.

Hofstede, G. (1980). *Culture's consequences: International differences in work-related values*. Beverly Hills, CA: Sage.

Hofstede, G. (1991). *Cultures and organizations: Software of the mind*. London: McGraw-Hill.

Industrial Cooperative Association (1985). *Mondragón: An English language bibliography*. Sommerville, MA: ICA.

Informe económico financiero de Andalucía [Financial and economic report on Andalucía] (1989, 1990, 1991). Junta de Andalucía.

Lee, C. W. (1990) . Relative status of employees and styles of handling interpersonal conflict: An experimental study with Korean managers. *International Journal of Conflict Management, 1*, 327–340.

Martín-Domingo, M. C. (1985). Algunas conclusiones a la luz de los estudios experimentales sobre el proceso de negociación [Conclusions in view of experimental studies on the process of negotiation]. In *Presente y futuro de la psicología del trabajo en la empresa* [Present and future of work psychology in companies] (pp. 139–144). Madrid: Fundación Universidad-Empresa.

McClelland, D. C. (1961). *The achievement society*. Princeton, NJ: D. Van Nostrand.

Meliá, J. L., & Peiró, J. M. (1985). Análisis empírico de un modelo bifactorial de poder e influencia en las organizaciones [Empirical analysis of a two factor model of power and influence in organizations]. *Proceedings of the Second National Congress on Work Psychology: Book of Papers* (pp. 243–302). Tarrasa: Universidad Autónoma de Barcelona.

Mohrman, S. A., Ledford, G. E., Lawler, E. E., & Mohrman, A. M. (1986). Quality of worklife and employee involvement. In C. L. Cooper & I. T. Robertson (Eds.), *International review of industrial and organizational psychology* (pp. 217–234). Chichester: Wiley.

Mondragón Experiment (1986). Mondragón: Caja Laboral Popular.

Munduate, L. (1987a). La aproximación negociadora al análisis de las organizaciones sociales [The negotiation approach to the analysis of social organizations]. *Boletín de Psicología, 15*, 23–40.

Munduate, L. (1987b) . El proceso de negociación en las organizaciones [The process of negotiation in organizations]. *Temas Laborales, 12*, 25–47.

Munduate, L. (1988). Poder y política en las organizaciones [Power and politics in organizations]. *First Latin American Congress and Third National Congress on Work and Organizational Psychology: Book of Conferences* (pp. 72–79). Madrid: Colegio de Psicólogos.

Munduate, L. (1992). *Psicosociologia de las relaciones laborales* [Psychosociology of industrial relations]. Barcelona: Promociones y Publicaciones Universitarias (PPU).

Munduate, L., & Barón, M. (1990). Algunas consideraciones psicosociales sobre la negociación colectiva [Some social psychological considerations about collective bargaining]. *Third National Congress on Social Psychology: Book of Symposia* (pp. 120–131). Santiago: Tórculo.

Munduate, L., Ganaza, J., & Alcaide, M. (1993). Estilos de gestión del conflicto interpersonal en las organizaciones [Styles of handling interpersonal conflict in organizations]. *Revista de Psicología Social, 8* (1), 47–68.

Orizo, F. A. (1991). *Los valores de los españoles* [Values in Spain]. Madrid: Fundación Santa María.

Ortega y Gasset, J. (1921) . *España invertebrada.* [Nonvertebrate Spain]. Madrid: Calpe.

Ortega y Gasset, J. (1983) . *José Ortega y Gasset: Obras Completas* [. . . : Complete works]. Madrid: Alianza.

Osorio, M. (1992). *El directivo en Europa* [The manager in Europe]. Ingenieros Consultores, S.A. (ICSA), internal paper.

Papeles de Economía Española (1989). *La empresa privada en España* [The private organization in Spain]. Madrid, Vol. 39–40.

Peiró, J. M. & Munduate, L. (1994). Work and organizational psychology in Spain. *Applied Psychology: An International Review, 42* (2), 171–189.

Pérez-Velasco, V. M. (1985) . Jerarquía de valores profesionales en mandos intermedios [The hierarchy of professional values among intermediate executives]. *Proceedings of the Second National Congress on Work Psychology: Book of Papers* (pp. 111–120). Tarrasa: Universidad Autónoma de Barcelona.

Porat, A. M. (1969). Cross-cultural differences in resolving union-management conflict through negotiations. *Experimental Publications System, 2,* 069A.

Quijano de Arana, S. D. (1982). *Ideología organizacional y conflicto laboral* [Organizational ideology and industrial conflict]. Summary of doctoral dissertation. Barcelona: Centre de Publicaciones, Universitat de Barcelona.

Racionero, L. (1985) . El Mediterraneo y los bárbaros del norte [The Mediterranean and the barbarians from the north]. Barcelona: Laia.

Rahim, M. A. (1983a). *Rahim Organizational Conflict Inventory–II: Forms A, B, & C.* Palo Alto, CA: Consulting Psychologists Press.

Rahim, M. A. (1983b). A measure of styles of handling interpersonal conflict. *Academy of Management Journal, 26,* 368–376.

Rahim, M. A. (1985). A strategy for managing conflict in complex organizations. *Human Relations, 38,* 81–89.

Rahim, M. A. (1986) . Referent role and style of handling interpersonal conflict. *Journal of Social Psychology, 126,* 79–86.

Rahim, M. A. (1992). *Managing conflict in organizations* (2nd ed.). Westport, CT: Praeger.

Rahim, M. A., & Bonoma, T. V. (1979). Managing organizational conflict: A model for diagnosis and intervention. *Psychological Reports, 44,* 1323–1344.

Remeseiro, C., & Méndez, T. (1988). Estrategias y tácticas en convenios colectivos. Diferencias entre empresarios y trabajadores [Strategies and tactics in collective bargaining. Differences between management and workers]. *First Latin American Congress and Third National Congress on Work and Organizational Psychology: Book of Papers* (pp. 279–283). Madrid: Colegio de Psicólogos.

Rey, S. (1992). *La resolución extrajudicial de conflictos colectivos laborales.* [The nonjudicial ways of resolution of laboral conflicts]. Sevilla: Consejo Andaluz de Relaciones Laborales.

Rodríguez, J. L. (1990). El proceso de negociación colectiva a través del enfoque dramatúrgico. [The collective bargaining process from the theatrical approach]. In J. Peiró (Dir.), *Trabajo, organizaciones y marketing social* [Work, organizations and social marketing] (pp. 113–118), Barcelona: Promociones y Publicaciones Universitarias (PPU).

Serrano, G. (1987a). La negociación colectiva: Dimensiones psicosociales [Collective bargaining: Social psychological dimensions]. *Revista de Psicología del Trabajo y de las Organizaciones, 3,* 7–19.

Serrano, G. (1987b) . La mediación en los procesos de negociación: Un estudio experimental [Mediation in negotiation: An experimental study]. *Revista de Psicología Social, 1,* 137–152.

Serrano, G. (1988) . La eficacia de los procesos de negociación [Effectiveness of negotiation]. *First Latin American Congress and Third National Congress on Work and Organizational Psychology. Book of Symposia* (pp. 87–92). Madrid: Colegio de Psicólogos.

Serrano, G. (1990) . Procesos cognitivos y negociación [Cognitive processes and negotiation]. *Third National Congress on Social Psychology. Book of Symposia* (pp. 168–182). Santiago: Tórculo.

Serrano, G., & Remeseiro, C. (1987) . Actitudes ante la negociación colectiva [Attitudes toward collective bargaining]. *Boletín de Psicología, 14,* 79–108.

Stephenson, G. M., & Brotherton, C. J. (Eds). (1979). *Industrial relations: A social psychological approach,* Chichester: Wiley.

Thomas, H., & Logan, C. (1980). *Mondragón: An economic analysis.* London: Allen & Urwin.

Van De Vliert, E., & Kabanoff, B. (1990). Toward theory-based measures of conflict management. *Academy of Management Journal, 33,* 199–209.

Vidal Abascal, V. (1991). *La gestión empresarial en los años 90* [The business management in the 90s]. Burson-Marsteller, Spain. Internal paper.

Weider-Hatfield, D. (1988). Assessing the Rahim Organizational Conflict Inventory–II (ROCI–II). *Management Communication Quarterly, 1,* 350–366.

8

TURKEY

M. Kamil Kozan

Open and direct handling of conflict is one of the troublesome aspects of Turkish work life. This can be observed in labor relations practice where difficulties in conflict management by the parties have invited state intervention on a regular basis. An aversion to confrontational tactics also pervades organizational life. Conflict within the organization is seen as a threat to harmony. Use of authority is, therefore, justified to subsume conflict and maintain a peaceful work climate.

Third-party intervention is often used to lessen the tension associated with confrontational behaviors. This involves both arbitration and mediation. Interorganizational conflict such as labor-management stalemates are mostly handled through arbitration. On the other hand, mediation has been found to elicit problem-solving and compromising behaviors from disputants within organizations. One of the more promising avenues for improved conflict management may be skillful use of mediational practices.

This chapter discusses both conflict management styles and third-party roles in Turkish organizations. Description of styles is primarily based on a survey of managers in public and private organizations. The reporting of the empirical study is preceded by reviews of the cultural, social, and economic milieus; the legal framework of employment relationships; and managerial styles. A later section provides additional survey results on third-party roles of managers in handling subordinates' conflicts. Wherever possible, comparisons are made to the findings on conflict management styles of managers in the United States.

SOCIAL, CULTURAL, AND ECONOMIC FACTORS

Turkey is located between the Middle East and the Balkan and Black Sea regions. It has a territory of approximately 300,000 square miles and a population close to 60 million. The population growth rate is high at 2.5 per thousand, resulting in a young population with 38.5 percent at the age of fourteen or below. Concentration is in a few large cities (with Istanbul over 10 million) and the numerous agriculturally rich lowlands along the country's coast. The population is racially heterogenous; Turks, of Central Asian origin, have blended with the earlier inhabitants of Anatolia and, later, with northern peoples from the Balkans and the Caucasus.

Turkey has shown a continuous effort for a century and a half to modernize its traditional society. The impetus for change has largely come from above, with intellectuals, the military, and civil bureaucrats pressing hard for the westernization of the country. Most notable is the establishment of secular laws and education after the founding of the republic in 1923. Its maintenance has been a formidable task in a country with a population that is 98 percent mostly devout Muslims and where the tide of the Islamic resurgence movement has swept the region recently.

Today, the more westernized segments of the society are markedly different in their values and life-styles than the rural population or city dwellers with a rural origin. Even the westernized groups sometimes carry a duality of Western and Middle Eastern attitudes and values with regard to the various facets of society, ranging from the role of women in society to authority relations at work. Significant differences may exist between the formally prescribed, mostly Western, norms and the informal, traditional ways.

As part of the modernization efforts, a heavy emphasis has been placed on industrialization. A mixed economic model has been used to achieve this goal; both private and state-owned enterprises are heavily involved in economic activity, although the scale has started to tip in favor of the former in recent years. Approximately half of the industry is run by the private sector, including manufacture of durable goods, automobiles, textiles, and food processing. The state's involvement in the economy extends to public utilities, mining, and certain manufacturing areas such as steel, petrochemicals, paper, textiles, and machinery.

Private-sector companies, most of which are family controlled, have to work in close cooperation with the state. They depend for their inputs on state-run industries and import quotas regulated by the government. Furthermore, they operate in a heavily protected environment created by import restrictions and export incentives. A good proportion of private-sector managers have gained their early work experiences in state-owned firms or government agencies. Good relations with the government are key to success for these firms.

Medium to large formal organizations are heavily concentrated in industry and services such as banking. The role of industry has steadily increased in the economy in general, and in exports in particular. Nearly half of the $52 billion gross domestic product (GDP) comes from manufacturing and mining, construction, and transportation and utilities. The shares of services and agriculture each account for about one-fifth of the GDP. The agricultural sector, which employs more than half of the population, is mainly comprised of small, scattered enterprises.

Rapid industrialization, accompanied by heavy immigration to the cities and rising aspirations, has created strains in relations among the social strata and in the political process. Labor-management relations have been a particularly troublesome area. The multiparty democratic system has also been torn apart by intense conflict between parties with right- and left-wing inclinations. Social unrest and parliamentary gridlock caused by intransigent leaders led to three military interventions since the inception of multiparty democracy in 1946. While the parliamentary system was restored each time, showing a commitment to democracy, the difficulties associated with the democratic process in the Turkish culture seemed evident.

Underlying these difficulties is the lack of a political culture capable of compromise on a consistent basis. The Turkish parliamentary system has been plagued by difficulties in the formation and maintenance of effective coalitions, which were often necessitated by the inability of any single party to secure the absolute majority in congress. The military coup of 1980 actually followed a period during which political parties were unable to come to terms with each other in the face of widespread violence among underground political factions. The election law in effect today provides a parlimentary majority to a party that receives as low as 30 percent of the popular vote. A major challenge that still faces Turkish democracy is the establishment of a problem-solving and compromising political culture capable of functioning without the heavy-handed third-party role of the military.

Attitudes toward confrontation in this culture are basically negative; open conflict is seen as harmful and something to be avoided. Turks have difficulty in aggressively defending their interests on a face-to-face basis without jeopardizing the existing relationship. When dissatisfied with another person's actions, they would rather keep silent or complain to others than directly confront the offender. Open conflict, on the other hand, is accompanied by a nonreconciliatory attitude and harsh language.

Mediators play a crucial role in conflict management because of the cultural aversions to direct confrontation. Starr (1978) describes in detail how Turkish villagers handle their disputes through mediators. Informal mediation is preferred to litigation because courts can seldom go into the finest details of a case. They often produce decisions that, although in strict accordance with the law codes, usually leave one or more of the litigants unsatisfied. Complex disputes may need more than one lawsuit, as dissatisfied litigants return to court with new complaints.

The villagers prefer to negotiate through representatives who lend their weight to one side or the other (but one side only), although, of course, they usually are not as partial and short-sighted about a situation as the principal they represent. Thus, by their presence, they tend to inject a certain amount of "good sense" into the process and sometimes enter into hard negotiation as well (Starr, 1978, p. 136).

The roots of the difficulty with direct confrontation may perhaps be found in the socialization process. The father's authority over his children is absolute, and its contention is no light matter. Bradburn (1963) found that few of the businessmen he interviewed in Turkey had ever argued with their fathers, and those who had did so at the price of an open break. The authoritarian climate that begins at home is reinforced through schooling in youth and a long mandatory military service for men in early adulthood. This upbringing fosters submission, or rebellion in extreme cases, more than it helps develop the emotions associated with negotiation and compromise. As Dereli (1968) states,

As long as there is a third party, such as the mother, as a reconciling figure in the presence of an authoritarian father or the government in conciliating the labor-management conflict, through which the parties can channel their dissatisfaction in an indirect way, the direct expression of conflict remains suppressed and disguised (pp. 51–52).

In addition to the cultural factors, one needs to look at the legal context within which employment relations, including conflictful ones, take shape in organizations. Turkey has a code-law system that replaced the Islamic laws of the *ancien regime* during the 1920s. Relevant for our discussion are the French-based Labor Code, the Law of Obligations (a replica of the Swiss equivalent), and the commercial code, which jointly provide the legal context within which individual employment relations are conducted. Managers' employment relations fall within this legal framework. Certain collective bargaining clauses may also be relevant in conflicts involving individuals. But in practice managerial personnel are usually excluded from collective bargaining agreements. The nonhourly employees of state enterprises are subject to special laws.

Conflicts between individual employees and their employers in the private sector over rights issues (i.e., those not involving wage negotiation) are subject mainly to the provisions of the Labor Code. These conflicts are ultimately settled in labor courts. The Labor Code makes no distinction between blue- or white-collar workers, and managerial personnel are subject to the same provisions as are hourly workers. Legally, an employment contract creates a dependency relationship between the employee (including a manager) and the employer, in which the employee accepts working under a hierarchy of authority. Written organizational policies and procedures are enforceable even when not mentioned in the employment contract, as long as the employee does not have any objections to them at the start of employment (Celik, 1988).

Employment of white-collar government employees and managers in the public sector is subject to the Government Employees Law and special laws for the trial of government employees. A government employee has tenure after a one- to two-year probationary period. Termination of tenured personnel is possible after repeated poor performance appraisals and actions by disciplinary committees at several levels. Separate administrative courts exist, organized hierarchically from local ones up to the Council of State.

State-owned enterprises are highly centralized and formalized. Superiors' orders are to be carried out under all conditions. A subordinate may object to an order if its legality is in doubt. In such cases, the order still has to be carried out if the superior repeats the order in writing and assumes responsibility (Turkiye ve Orta, 1988). Subordinates have the rights to complaint and to take legal action concerning their superiors' actions.

A progressive discipline system exists, implemented by the immediate supervisor when reprimands and salary cuts are involved, and by disciplinary committees at different levels for denial of merit increases or termination of employment (Tortop, 1987). Subordinates may object to disciplinary action of superiors through committees and up through the Council of State.

As the foregoing description demonstrates, the legal frameworks within which managerial personnel are employed in the private and public sectors are different in their comprehensiveness and detail. Elaborate laws and bylaws exist for the manager working in the public sector. Managers working in the private sector, on the other hand, have little legal guidelines with regard to resolving their individual disputes with superiors, dealing with disciplinary action, or the process of termination of their employment. In spite of these differences, though, the legal context in both private and public firms emphasizes and protects the authority of the manager.

MANAGERIAL STYLES

The managerial styles in Turkish organizations, private and public, have been described as predominantly autocratic. Hofstede's (1983) data from IBM subsidiary employees have placed Turkey high among forty other countries in power distance. The power distance index reflects a lack of participative style on the part of managers and a relatively low preference for participative managers by the employees. More important, the index reflects the degree to which subordinates are "afraid to express disagree-

ment with their managers" (Hofstede, 1983, p. 73). Other research findings
are in agreement with Hofstede's data. In a study of sixteen firms in
Turkey, eight of which were subsidiaries of U.S. firms, Lauter (1968) found
that committees were used to a limited degree, with final decisions re-
served for top management or headquarters. Top managers explained that
it was difficult to generate discussion and get new ideas.

Hofstede (1983) has found strong uncertainty avoidance for Turkey, reflecting a need for rules and employment stability. This result should be interpreted more as a sign of concern for security than adherence to strict
bureaucratic norms. Hofstede also reports that Turkey is relatively low in
individualism. A low score in this dimension shows a local as opposed to
a cosmopolitan attitude, emphasizing loyalty to organization rather than
personal achievement. In the fourth and final dimension, which Hofstede
labels as masculinity, the Turkish employees scored relatively low. This dimension measures work values that stress challenge, advancement, and
earnings (masculine values) as opposed to relations, security, and location
of employment (feminine values).

Low individualism and masculinity and high uncertainty avoidance,
when coupled with high power distance, mix well to create a warm but
autocratic organizational climate. "The firm is viewed as a family with the
employees as children and the manager the authoritarian father" (Bradburn, 1963, p. 63). This climate fosters a "benevolent autocratic" management style, which fits the employees' expectations of their managers well.

Strong managers are the main mechanism of control and coordination.
Little emphasis is placed on various informal means of coordination that
may threaten the formal authority of the manager. For example, cliques
are seen as essentially harmful; the recognition of such groups as sources
to be influenced toward accomplishment of organizational objectives is
an alien idea to these managers (Lauter, 1968). Furthermore, a separation
exists between different levels of managers. In none of the firms Lauter
studied could a systematic attempt to develop a cohesive group of managers be observed. Needless to say, such attempts would require team-
building and group decision-making, practices that are at odds with an
emphasis on status and power differentials between superiors and subordinates.

Turkish managers treat authority as belonging to their person rather
than position alone. The manager is always in role and has to be treated
with respect in informal settings, as well. Formal appearance and measured behaviors are essential in reinforcing these concerns. A manager's
effectiveness is seen as closely tied to respect received from subordinates.

The actual achievement of control is another matter, though. Centralized
decision-making does not necessarily mean effective control. Turkish management practice is also plagued by control that exists only in appearance,
an administrative problem in all Third World countries (Milne, 1970).

Managers are not as persistent in implementing and following up on decisions as in having them initially accepted.

STYLES OF HANDLING INTERPERSONAL CONFLICT

Having briefly described the cultural and legal setting within which Turkish organizations function, we now turn to the discussion of the results of a survey of managers with respect to their styles of handling conflicts. Conflict occurs in several forms in an organization, including conflict between individuals or groups and conflict involving more than two parties (coalitions). The present survey was concerned with conflicts between managers. The study used a model of five conflict management styles comprised of integrating, obliging, dominating, avoiding, and compromising.

A manager's tendency to use one or another style has been shown to be influenced by a number of variables, including personality, the reward structure, and rules in the firm governing decision-making once conflict arises (Thomas, 1976). The present study examines how preferences for the styles differ in relation to a number of variables. A case has been made above for differences in the private and public sectors. Hence, relation of private versus state ownership of the organization to the styles used was investigated.

The authority position of the other party—that is, whether he or she is a superior, peer, or subordinate—was also included as a variable in the study. Rahim's (1986) survey of U.S. managers has shown the position power of the other party to affect the style used, with managers appearing to be more obliging with superiors, integrating with subordinates, and compromising with peers. The constraining effects of hierarchy of authority on conflict styles would be expected to be as potent a factor in Turkey. As mentioned earlier, the Turkish culture is known for high power distance between superior and subordinate. Centralized decision-making and strong, authoritarian leadership seem to be characteristic of Turkish organizations (Ronen, 1986; Lauter, 1968). We may expect a more dominating and less integrating style toward subordinates in Turkey than in the United States.

Data were collected from managers in fourteen private and eight public organizations in Istanbul (the industrial and commercial center of the country) and Ankara (the capital and second largest city). The sample included four firms in electronics manufacturing; three in each of metal manufacturing, food processing, and utilities; two in each of construction and banking; and one in each of plastics, textiles, shipping, distribution, and broadcasting. When compared to the industry distribution of GDP discussed earlier, this sample seems to overrepresent manufacturing (half of the managers in the sample) and underrepresent agriculture (none, if food processing firms are excluded).

In firms with more than twelve managers a random sample of twelve managers was chosen, while in smaller firms all of the managers were included in the study. As a result, 259 managers were contacted, and usable returns were obtained from 215 (83 percent). Ninety-three of the respondents worked for state-owned enterprises and 122 for the private sector. The sample was 93 percent male, with an average age of forty-one. Those with a college education or higher constituted 85 percent of the sample. Among the college graduates, 39 percent had degrees in engineering and 40 percent in business and economics. Top-level managers accounted for 22 percent of the respondents, middle-level managers for 60 percent, and first-level supervisors for 18 percent.

Data were collected by means of a questionnaire. Each of the five styles of handling interpersonal conflict was measured by a statement adopted from the Rahim Organizational Conflict Inventory (ROCI–II) (Rahim, 1983a). Each statement was worded so as to represent, as much as possible within a sentence, the behaviors depicted for a style in the multi-item ROCI–II. These statements, representing (1) integrating, (2) obliging, (3) dominating, (4) avoiding, and (5) compromising, are as follows:

(1) I try to bring all of my and his or her concerns out in the open and work for a solution together.

(2) I try to accommodate his or her wishes.

(3) I am firm in my position and use my power to get my view accepted.

(4) I stay away from disagreement and avoid open discussion of differences.

(5) I propose a solution halfway between my and his or her wishes to break any deadlock.

The respondents were asked to recall two recent conflict situations that involved "performance appraisal and salaries." They then indicated how well each of the style statements described their behavior on a dichotomous response scale (agree or disagree). This procedure was repeated for three additional conflict topics: "proper performance of responsibilities and rule compliance," "work methods to be used and implementation of plans," and "personal habits, mannerisms, and values."

The use of a single item for each style made repetition and measurement over various conflict topics possible, as well as the calculation of a composite style score covering those topics. The results should be interpreted with some caution though, as reliability coefficients could not be calculated for the single item measures.

The questionnaires were translated into Turkish and retranslated into English to ensure reliability by bilingual colleagues of the author. The respondents filled out the questionnaires alone during work hours at their place of work and the anonymity of responses was assured.

Three different sets of questionnaires were administered, each one involving a different party to the conflict—subordinate, peer, or superior. A respondent randomly received only one of these sets, which identified, at the beginning and when each topic was introduced, who the party to the conflict was.

The questionnaire was tested for social desirability bias by means of a twenty-item scale developed for Turkey (Kozan, 1983). Based on the principles used by Crowne and Marlowe (1960), this scale contained items that described socially desirable but improbable behaviors. None of the correlations between the social desirability scale and the five conflict styles was significant at the .05 level. Hence, self-reports of conflict behavior were not influenced by the respondents' tendencies to give socially desirable answers.

Data analysis was carried out by a multivariate analysis of variance. Position power and ownership were between subjects factors. The dependent variables were the frequency by which each style was used. This design allowed for testing differences among the five styles in general, effect of position power of the other party on style, effect of state versus private ownership on style, and interaction effects involving the above factors. Where this analysis yielded significant results, discriminant analyses were conducted to find out more about the effect in question.

In general, managers preferred some styles over others. Paired comparisons among means of the styles showed that managers used collaborating significantly (p < .05) more often than dominating and compromising. These latter two were used more often than avoiding, which, in turn, was used more often than the least likely style, obliging.

No significant difference was found in style preferences between managers working for the private sector or state-owned enterprises. On the other hand, preferences for the different styles were affected by the authority position of the other party. No interaction effect was found. Table 8.1 gives the means and standard deviations for managers' styles with superior(s), subordinates, and peers.

In order to determine which styles were associated with different authority positions (a between-subjects factor), a discriminant analysis was run. The discriminant analysis used a stepwise selection procedure, utilizing Mahallanobis distance as selection criteria. The canonical discriminant functions were rotated using the varimax method.

The analysis yielded two significant discriminant functions with Chi-square coefficients of 58.85 (p < .001) and 13.01 (p < .01). After rotation, the two discriminant functions correctly classified 50 percent of the cases (chance alone would have yielded 33 percent correct classification). As shown in Table 8.2, the styles that distinguish conflict handling with respect

Table 8.1
**Means and Standard Deviations (in parentheses) for Conflict Management
Styles (Turkey) (N = 215)***

	Overall	Conflict with		
		Superior	Peer	Subordinate
Integrating	3.87 (2.31)	4.13 (2.41)	3.93 (2.40)	3.56 (2.11)
Obliging	.82 (1.44)	1.46 (1.98)	.56 (.99)	.45 (.87)
Dominating	1.70 (1.82)	1.08 (1.37)	1.38 (1.69)	2.61 (1.98)
Avoiding	1.08 (1.49)	1.50 (1.64)	1.42 (1.83)	1.31 (2.11)
Compromising	1.59 (1.84)	1.85 (2.07)	1.44 (1.64)	1.48 (1.80)

Note: The scores represent the number of times a particular style was used in a total of eight recent conflict
episodes recalled by the respondent.

to position of other party in Turkey are dominating toward subordinates, obliging toward superiors, and, to a lesser degree, avoiding toward peers.

These findings and evidence from other studies suggest the following profile for Turkish managers in each of the five conflict-handling styles. Comparisons made with U.S. managers are based on survey results reported by Rahim (1983b, 1986).

Integrating

An integrating approach is the most preferred style. In this regard, Turkish managers may not be different from their counterparts in other countries. For example, integrating is also the most popular style with managers in the United States. A difference between Turkish and U.S. managers emerged when conflicts involved subordinates, however. Conflict with subordinates in the United States is distinguished by increased integrating behavior. This was not the case with Turkish managers.

An integrative approach involves high levels of both assertiveness and cooperation. Managers in Turkey fear that an integrative, problem-solving approach toward an assertive subordinate will be taken as a sign of weakness by the subordinate and onlookers. As Bradburn (1963, p. 66) has observed, "any breakdown of the behavior pattern which characterizes the superior-subordinate relationship, would tend to destroy the respect on which authority is based."

Table 8.2
Discriminant Analysis Results (Turkey) (N = 215)

	Rotated Canonical Discriminant Functions	
	Function 1	Function 2
Correlation with Discriminant Variables:		
Integrating	-.12	.05
Obliging	-.11	.84
Dominating	.94	-.15
Avoiding	-.44	-.48
Compromising	-.12	-.24
Discriminant Scores for Party:		
Subordinates	.53	-.25
Peers	-.24	-.26
Superiors	-.29	.52

Obliging

To be accommodative of the other party's wishes is the least common style, according to the managers' self-reports. In comparison, U.S. managers ranked obliging as the third most common style. A concern for face-saving, which is common in Eastern cultures, is undoubtedly a factor in the undesirability of obliging.

Despite its undesirability, obliging is the only style that is used significantly more when a manager is in conflict with a superior. These managers were clearly less assertive toward their superiors. It may be recalled from our earlier discussion of Hofstede's (1983) research that Turkey is relatively high in power distance between superior and subordinate, which reflected "employees' fear of expressing disagreement with their managers" and lack of participation in decision-making. When encouraged to participate, subordinates expect top managers to make propositions and then limit their participation only to identify possible problem areas without, however, directly contradicting their executives (Lauter, 1968).

Dominating

Dominating tied for second place in managers' self-reports, an unusually high ranking in comparison to the United States, where it was ranked last. Unlike the United States, dominating furthermore distinguished the handling of conflicts with a subordinate. These findings reflect the prevalent authoritarian tone of administration in the Turkish culture. Most managers believe that to be in control, they have to be firm toward disagreeing subordinates. To preserve the authority relationship, any concessions made to a subordinate must come after the superior has asserted himself and an obliging response has been secured.

Avoiding

This is one of the least preferred styles by Turkish managers. Particularly in superior-subordinate conflict, parties like to see the conflict resolved. An ongoing, constant state of conflict is seen as harmful to organizational harmony and effectiveness. Use of avoiding somewhat distinguished conflict among peers. In this regard, Turkish managers may not be standing alone; managers in the United States, for example, have also been found to resort to avoiding with peers. Given the hierarchic nature of most organizations, interdependency—that is, the stakes involved—is higher between superiors and subordinates than among peers.

Compromising

In the United States, compromising is the second most preferred style after integrating. Compromise may be a fall-back option if the first style is inappropriate or is not working (Blake & Mouton, 1964). Compromise was also the second most common style with Turkish managers; however, it tied for second place with forcing. The ambivalence of Turkish managers for compromise is evident in these results. On the one hand, bargaining and give-and-take are acknowledged as the only path to resolution of some conflicts. On the other hand, compromise represents lack of principles or integrity of position (or even of character).

The stylistic patterns described above were not significantly different for private and state-owned organizations. Other researchers have also found evidence for a rather homogeneous managerial philosophy across Turkish organizations. Lauter (1968) found the same paternalistic managerial attitude for both the Turkish and U.S. subsidiary firms that he studied. Heper (1977) reported a mixture of "patrimonial" and "legal-bureaucratic" tendencies to be uniform across government agencies dealing with technical tasks and those dealing with the more traditional, administrative tasks.

Differences in legal environment, which were pronounced between the public and private sectors, seem to have had little effect on conflict behavior. Rather, cultural factors, springing from a series of socialization experiences in the family, school, and military service, offer an explanation for the similarity of conflict profiles in the two sectors. By the time they begin their work careers in private firms or in government, these young men have learned how to function under a benevolent-autocratic style. In addition, private-sector managers are heavily recruited from among those working for state-owned enterprises. Making their moves in midcareer for middle or top management posts, they also play a role in bringing managerial practices in the two sectors closer together.

ALTERNATIVE DISPUTE MANAGEMENT

When the authority element is removed, parties that enter into open conflict in this culture have a problem thereafter in adopting a conciliatory, compromising attitude. This difficulty manifests itself in several facets of Turkish society, including industrial relations and organizational behavior, as well as the political arena as discussed earlier. The remedy is usually sought in alternative dispute resolution through third parties.

Labor-management relations is an area where the law calls for strong third-party involvement to overcome difficulties in conflict management. The Labor Union Law and the Collective Bargaining, Strikes, and Lockouts Act are quite restrictive and rely heavily on the government as a third party. General strikes and lockouts, as well as those that have political or solidarity purposes, are outlawed. The law stipulates that mediation is required before a strike can be legal. If the collective bargaining process fails to bring agreement within sixty days, a mediator is automatically assigned. Mediators are chosed randomly by the government from an official list.

The law also provides for arbitration by mutual consent of the parties. Arbitration is mandatory in special cases where strikes may be harmful to public welfare, including utilities, urban transportation, banks, and hospitals. Arbitration is also mandatory if the government decides to postpone strikes or lockouts for "public health" or "security" reasons and no agreement is reached within sixty days. Arbitration is exclusively carried out by a special council, headed by the head of the labor relations division of the Council of State, and is composed of representatives from the government, the largest labor union confederation and employers' confederation, and labor relations experts chosen by the government and the state-run universities (Celik, 1988). The council's composition clearly gives the government a dominant role in settling disputes delegated to it, including those involving the state-owned enterprises where the government itself is a party to the conflict. As Danis (1989) has observed, the state is indeed a regular party in industrial relations conflicts in Turkey. The legal arrangements for this purpose may, in part, be a reflection of the difficulty labor and management have had in establishing an effective conflict-resolution process between themselves.

Third-party roles constitute a strong alternative to direct interpersonal conflict management within organizations, too. However, this is not achieved through institutionalized mediation or arbitration methods, except for the formalized appeals system in the government. The ombudsman role is also an alien concept. In private firms, personnel managers are "responsible" on paper for the handling of disputes with the exception of those involving higher management. In practice, however, their role is confined to disciplinary action pertaining to the rank and file. Line managers are the main group of actors that play the crucial third-party roles in conflicts among those working under them.

A recent survey of 300 managers investigated the type of third-party roles played by their superiors (Kozan and Ilter, 1992). Factor analysis of items drawn from the work of Karambayya and Brett (1989) and Kolb (1986) yielded essentially similar third-party role categories. Among these, mediation was found to be the most commonly used role. Next came the role of the restructurer, which refers to a manager who changes organizational structure, such as assignment of duties and reporting relations, in order to facilitate resolution of disputes. The laissez-faire style, which left the parties on their own, and autocratic intervention were the least commonly used roles.

Mediation by managers in the third-party role resulted in more integration and compromise behavior on the part of the disputants. The latter also reported that the conflict was more effectively managed. In contrast, autocratic intervention by the third party stimulated more dominating behavior from the disputants, and conflict resolution was seen as less effective.

Although dominating when in conflict with a subordinate, Turkish managers assume more of a peacemaker style in a third-party role. The threat to personal authority is apparently removed when the person is not the target of the dispute. The culture also bestows stature to the peacemaker, who is above the disputants and working for the common good rather than self-interest.

Even more significant was the finding that the disputants become more integrating and compromising when they get help. The presence of intermediaries enables parties to save face in abandoning an intransigent stance or making concessions. Mediators, working separately with each party, can soften them and bring a more conciliatory attitude by appealing to the virtues of forgiveness and benevolence. When left on their own (i.e., when a third party played the laissez-faire role), the managers surveyed indicated less use of integrating and compromising.

DISCUSSION

Turkish managers' proficiency in the use of the dominating style toward subordinates may be a mixed blessing. As Lawrence and Lorsch (1967) have argued, dominating may be necessary as a backup mode for getting results. It may also serve as a unifying force in the organizations and prove to be effective, especially in crisis situations. On the other hand, cooperation may be hard to achieve in the absence of strong leaders. Furthermore, the maintenance of undisputed authority turns into a topmost priority for the Turkish executive. As a consequence, "the primary focus of role evaluation is placed on the ability to control others, rather than on the ability to achieve the goals of the organization" (Bradburn, 1963, p. 67).

The traditional view of conflict as harmful and something to be suppressed at any cost has changed during the past few decades. Robbins (1974) has argued that some organizations may indeed need conflict stimulation. Blake and Mouton (1964) have argued that if effectively managed through an integrating, problem-solving approach, conflicts may stimulate search for alternatives, innovation, and organizational adaptation. Through their overreliance on authority for resolving conflicts, managers in Turkey are not utilizing conflicts' potential to their fullest extent. More problem-solving with subordinates would be a welcome addition to these managers' repertory of styles.

Future research may have to look at the effects on the organization of the present conflict-management methods. One area worth investigating is how the difficulties in managing conflicts among peer managers affect horizontal coordination between their departments. Would overreliance on upper levels in handling such differences overload the hierarchy and reduce its effectiveness as Galbraith (1977) has suggested?

Further research is worth pursuing on third-party roles. This is an area particularly open to experimental research, which changes the type of third-party role played by managers. Such experimentation may profitably be extended to the schools and child-rearing practices, as the behavior patterns intended for change originate from these earlier socialization processes. The most promising approach to increasing integrative and compromising behaviors in this culture is the development of belief and skills in mediation for those in positions of authority.

Change in existing conflict-handling behaviors is likely to come slowly at best. Even in foreign subsidiaries operating in Turkey, it will be recalled, the managerial culture resembled that of other Turkish organizations. Foreigners doing business with their Turkish counterparts, or managers working in subsidiaries in Turkey, may have to take into account the aversion to open confrontation in this culture. Confrontation of managers in a superior position in particular may be counterproductive. It should be kept in mind that unlike managers in the United States, who received obliging responses in return for an integrating style, managers in Turkey were found to elicit obliging responses in return for a dominating style. Given the prevalent benevolent autocratic management styles, foreigners, as well as nationals, who function best in such a climate would have the least difficulty in managerial roles.

ACKNOWLEDGMENT

I would like to thank Dr. Kadir Varoglu for his invaluable assistance in the collection of the data on styles reported in this chapter.

REFERENCES

Blake, R. R., & Mouton, J. S. (1964). *The managerial grid*. Houston: Gulf.

Bradburn, N. (1963). Interpersonal relations in Turkish organizations. *Journal of Social Issues, 9* (1), 61–67.

Celik, N. (1988). *Is hukuku dersleri* [Labor law] Istanbul: Beta.

Crowne, D. P., & Marlowe, D. (1960). A new scale of social desirability independent of psychopathology. *Journal of Consulting Psychology, 24*, 349–354.

Danis, J. J. (1989). *The trade union movement in Turkey*. Brussels: European Trade Union Institute.

Dereli, T. (1968). *The development of Turkish trade unionism: A study of legislative and socio-political dimensions*. Istanbul: Istanbul University Press.

Galbraith, J. (1977). *Organizational design*. Reading, MA: Addison-Wesley.

Heper, M. (1977). *Turk kamu burokrasisinde gelenekcilik ve modernlesme* [Traditionalism and modernization in Turkish public bureaucracy]. Istanbul: Bogazici Universitesi Yayinlari.

Hofstede, G. (1983). National cultures in four dimensions. *International Studies of Management and Organization, 13* (2), 52.

Karambayya, R., & Brett, J. M. (1989). Managers handling disputes: Third party roles and perceptions of fairness. *Academy of Management Journal, 32*, 687–704.

Kolb, D. M. (1986). Who are organizational third parties, and what do they do? In R. J. Lewicki, B. H. Sheppard & M. H. Bazerman (Eds.), *Research on negotiation in organizations, 1*, 207–278.

Kozan, M. K. (1983). Davranis bilimleri arastirmalarinda sosyal begenirlik boyutu ve Turkiye icin bir sosyal begenirlik olcegi [The social desirability dimension in behavioral research and a social desirability scale for Turkish culture]. *METU Studies in Development, 10* (4), 447–477.

Kozan, M. K., & Ilter, S. (1992). Third-party roles of Turkish managers in subordinates' conflicts. Unpublished paper, St. John Fisher College, Rochester, NY.

Lauter, G. P. (1968). *An investigation of the applicability of modern management processes by industrial managers in Turkey*. Unpublished doctoral dissertation, University of California, Los Angeles, CA.

Lawrence, P. R. & Lorsch, J. W. (1967). *Organization and environment*. Homewood, IL: Irwin.

Milne, R. S. (1970). Mechanistic and organic models of public administration in developing countries. *Administrative Science Quarterly, 15*, 57–67.

Rahim, A. (1983a). A measure of styles of handling interpersonal conflict. *Academy of Management Journal, 26*, 368–376.

Rahim, A. (1983b). *Rahim Organizational Conflict Inventories: Professional manual*. Palo Alto, CA: Consulting Psychologists Press.

Rahim, A. (1986). Referent role and styles of handling interpersonal conflict. *Journal of Social Psychology, 125*, 79–86.

Robbins, S. P. (1974). *Managing organizational conflict: A nontraditional approach*. Englewood Cliffs, NJ: Prentice-Hall.

Ronen, S. (1986). *Comparative and multinational management*. New York: Wiley.

Starr, J. (1978). Turkish village disputing behavior. In L. Nader & H. F. Todd, Jr. (Eds.), *The disputing process: Law in ten societies* (pp. 122–151). New York: Columbia University Press.

Thomas, K. W. (1976). Conflict and conflict-management. In M. D. Dunette (Ed.), *Handbook of industrial and organizational psychology,* (pp. 889–935). Chicago: Rand-McNally.

Turkiye ve Orta Dgu Amme Idaresi Enstitusu (1988). *Devlet Memurlari El Kitabi* [Handbook for government employees]. Ankara: Todaie.

Tortop, N. (1987). *Kamu personel yonetimi* [Public personnel administration]. Ankara: Bilim Yay.

INDEX

Adam, H., 91
Alcaide, M., 103, 105, 106, 111, 116, 117, 121, 126, 129
Alexander, R. A., 115
Allen, J., 33
Alternative dispute management, 2, 25; arbitration, 104; conciliation, 104; France, 27–29; Japan, 47–49; judicial decisions, 122; mediation, 104; Netherlands, 61–63; Norway, 81–82; priority committees, 123–124; South Africa, 95–97; Spain, 122–124; Turkey, 147–148
Ando, T., 33
Anstey, M., 99
Anuario de Estadísticas Laborales, 123

Barnes, J. M., 69
Baron, M., 111
Barrett, G. K., 115
Barsoux, J.-L., 14, 16, 18, 20, 26
Bass, B. M., 115
Benedict, R., 38
Bergman, T. J., 125
Binnedell, N., 99
Blake, R. R., 4, 20, 127, 146, 149
Bluen, S., 89, 91
Blum, A. A., 1
Blunt, P., 93
Boada, F., 112, 114

Boissevain, J., 54
Bomers, G. B. J., 56
Bond, M. H., 59, 63
Bonoma, T. V., 4, 104, 127
Boulding, K. E., 6
Boyatziz, R. E., 91
Bradburn, N., 140, 144, 149
Bradley, K., 107
Brett, J. M., 67, 82, 148
Brotherton, C. J., 129
Buntzman, G. F., 4

Cádiz, A., 107, 111, 124, 128
Carment D. W., 59, 63
Carnevale, P. J., 128
Casado, D., 111
Celik, N., 139, 147
Comp-Langlois, H., 16, 20
Conflict, intrapersonal, 45; Japanese forms of, 35
Conflict management, styles, 1
—model of Japanese, 44; bottom-up decision-making, 41; *nemawashi*, 43; triadic management, 45
Cosier, R. A., 35
Cottaar, A., 53
Crowne, D. P., 143
Culture, constructs: cross-cultural ignorance, 33; *fait accompli* approach, 14; guilt, 38; individualism-collec-

tivism, 13, 36; low- and high-context, 13; monochronic-polychronic cultures, 13; shame, 38

Cura, J., 112, 114

Daalder, H., 54
Dalton, D. R., 35
Danis, J. J., 147
Dereli, T., 138
Deutsch, M., 7
Dickens, L., 128
D'Iribarne, P., 15, 17, 20, 23
Discussion at end of each chapter, 29–31, 49–50, 63–64, 97–100, 124–129
Dostal, E., 93
Drenth, P., 57, 60, 65

Elden, M., 70
Elias, N., 63
Emans, B., 53
Emdin, R., 93, 98
Emery, F. E., 70
Espina, A., 124
Exiga, A., 11, 20, 21

Factors, cultural dimensions: expert power, 2; feminine values, 4; individualism, 3; individualism-collectivism, 13, 36; masculinity, 3–4; masculinity-femininity, 36; power distance, 2, 36; tolerance of ambiguity, 2; uncertainty avoidance, 2, 14–15, 36, 140
—economic, social, and cultural, 1, 12–18, 104–112
—social, cultural, and economic, 1, 2–4, 35–39, 68–72, 87–91, 135–139
—vertical communications, 17
Fauvet, J. C., 21, 22, 26
Fennefoss, A., 73
Fernández-Ríos, M., 111, 123
Filella, J. C., 109, 115
Fisher, R., 67, 84, 92
Follett, M. P., 4, 6
Follett's rule, 6
Foster, D., 88
France, 3, 11–32

Fullagar, C., 89, 91

Galbraith, J., 149
Ganaza, J., 103, 116, 117, 121, 126, 129
Gao, G., 1, 4, 8, 13
García-Echevarría, S., 108, 109, 112, 113, 116, 119, 125
Geilb, A., 107
Ghiselli, E., 108, 114, 125
Giliomee, H., 90
Glossary of important [Japanese] terms, 50–51
Goguelin, P., 21, 30
Goldberg, S., 81, 82
Goldfield, M., 73
Goldman, A., 122
Gonzalez, J. L., 107
Gordon, R. J., 88
Goudsblom, J., 55
Green, E., 81
Greenwood, D., 107
Greiner, L., 98
Gruère, J. P., 12, 13, 14, 17, 18, 26
Gullestad, M., 78

Habert, K., 80
Haire, M., 108, 114, 125
Hall, E. T., 13, 18
Hall, M. R., 13, 18
Hartley, J., 129
Heller, F., 57, 60
Heper, M., 146
Hernández, J., 123
Herranz, R., 108, 110, 124
Hirschman, A. O., 72
Hofstede, G., 1, 2, 3, 4, 12, 13, 14, 16, 17, 20, 35, 58, 71, 85, 88, 89, 107–110, 115, 139, 140, 145
Horwitz, F. M., 87, 89, 93
Human, L., 90, 91
Human, P., 93

Icely, N., 90, 91
Ilter, S., 148
Industrial Cooperative Association, 107
Informe económico financiero de Andalucía, 106

Japan, 3, 34–51
Jubber, K., 88

Kabanoff, B., 4, 5, 7, 126
Kanter, R. M., 91
Karambayya, R., 148
Keenan, D., 4
Keenen, J., 88
Kelly, J., 129
Kiefer, P., 93
Kim, H. S., 1, 4, 8, 13
Kingmans, M. C., 56
Kipnis, D., 91
Klamer, A., 62
Klausen, A. M., 69, 79
Kolb, D. M., 148
Koopman, P., 57, 60
Kozan, M. K., 135, 143, 148
Krauss, E. S., 45
Kriesi, H., 54
Krishnan, L., 59, 63

Laskewitz, 53
Laurent, A., 17, 20
Lauter, G. P., 140, 141, 145, 146
Lawler, E. E., 128, 129
Lawrence, P., 14, 16, 18, 20, 26, 148
Lebel, P., 20, 21, 22, 24, 25, 27
Ledford, G., E., 128
Lee, C.-W., 4, 125
Lee, H. O., 12, 13
Leeds, C., 11
Leung, K., 59, 63
Levy, M. B., 4
Liebrand, W. B. G., 59, 63
Lijphart, A., 56
Lillebo, A., 80
Lin, S.-L., 1, 4, 8, 13
Linhart, D., 19
Logan, C., 107
Lorsch, J. W., 148

Maller, J., 94
Managerial styles, 1–2; benevolent au-
    tocrat, 140; collective, 19; commu-
    nicative, 19; consultative, 91;
    decoupling, 72; democratic, 91, 114;

dohki groups, 40–44; enlightened
    despots, 14; formalist, 113; France,
    19–21; Japan, 39–45 (lifetime em-
    ployment in, 40); modern, 19;
    Netherlands, 56–59 (depillarization,
    56; pillarization, 54); Norway, 72–75;
    participative, 19 (management sys-
    tem, 69); *ringi* system, 40–44; South
    Africa, 91–92; Spain, 113–116; tech-
    nocratic, 19; third-party intervention,
    72; Turkey, 139–141
Maree, J., 88
Marlowe, D., 143
Márquez, J. M., 112, 114
Martín-Domingo, M. C., 111
McClelland, D. C., 91, 109
McKersie, R. B., 7
Melía, J. L., 108, 113
Méndez, T., 115
Mohrman, A. M., 128, 129
Mohrman, S. A., 128, 129
Mole, J., 13, 29
Mondragón Cooperative Experience,
    107
Moodie, T. D., 88
Moran, R. T., 33, 47, 48, 49
Morel, P., 12, 13, 14, 17, 18, 26
Moulton, J. S., 4, 20, 127, 146, 149
Muller, D., 88
Munduate, L., 103, 105, 111, 112, 116,
    117, 121, 126, 129

Neff, E. K., 4
Negotiation, styles (strategies), 1; econ-
    omy, 69; of the Japanese and Ameri-
    cans, 48
Netherlands, the 3, 53–66
Nielsen, K., 70
Nishida, T., 1, 4, 8, 13
Norway, 3, 67–86
Nupen, C., 97

Odendaal, A., 88
Orizo, F. A., 104
Ortega y Gasset, J., 110
Osler, K., 93
Osorio, M., 117, 119

Papeles de Economía España, 113
Pedersen, O., 70
Peelen, G. J., 56
Peiró, J. M., 103, 105, 108, 111–113
Pérez, Yruela M., 111
Pérez-Velasco, V. M., 108, 110
Persico, J., Jr., 4
Pfeffer, J., 69
Philip, C., 88
Pilkington, C. J., 4
Piotet, F., 11, 20, 21
Porat, A. M., 108, 113
Porter, L. W., 108, 114, 125
Prein, H. C. M., 6
Pringle, H., 90
Pruitt, D. G., 7, 75, 76, 128
Psenicka, C., 4
Putnam, L. L., 7

Quijano de Arana, S. D., 111

Racionero, L., 109
Rahim, M. A., 1, 4, 7, 8, 67, 75, 85, 94,
    104, 116, 120, 121, 125, 126–129, 141,
    142, 144
Rahim Organizational Conflict Inven-
    tory–II, 8, 30, 116, 125–127, 142
Remeseiro, C., 115, 117, 120
Rey, S., 122–124
Richardson, D. R., 4
Rodríguez, J. L., 111
Rogan, R. G., 12, 13
Rognes, J. K., 67
Rohlen, T. P., 45
Rokkan, S., 69
Ronen, S., 141
Rosenstein, E., 57
Rubin, J., 75
Ruble, T. L., 5
Rus, V., 57, 60
Ryterband, F. C., 115

Sainsaulieu, R., 11, 20, 21, 27
Sander, F., 82
Sasano, M., 33
Savage, M., 88
Schein, E. H., 56

Schein, V., 98
Scholten, I., 56
Schwenk, C. R., 35
Senge, P., 93
Serrano, G., 111, 117, 120
Sheppard, B., 73, 75
Six, J. F., 28
South Africa, 3, 87–101
Spain, 3, 103–133
Starr, J., 137, 138
Steadman, F., 97
Steininger, R., 54
Steinhoff, P. G., 45
Stephenson, G. M., 129
Stoetzel, J., 56
Styles of handling interpersonal con-
    flict, 2, 4–9, 21–27, 45–47, 59–61,
    75–81, 93–95, 116–122, 141–147;
    avoiding, 6, 25–26, 45, 61, 78–80, 94,
    120, 146; compromising, 4–5, 7–9,
    26–27, 46, 61, 80–81, 95, 120–122,
    146–147; concern: for others, 3–9, for
    production, 3, for self, 3–9; country
    club leadership, 25; discriminant
    analysis results, 145; distributive di-
    mension, 7–9; dominating, 4–5, 25,
    47, 61, 77–78, 94, 119–120, 145–146;
    face-saving (*kao*), 45; forcing, 4; inte-
    grating, 4–6, 22–23, 46, 60, 75–76, 93,
    117–119, 144–145; integrative dimen-
    sion, 7–9; lose-lose, 7; lose-win, 7;
    managerial reference group norms,
    117–122; means and standard devia-
    tions, 144; mixed, 7; negative-sum, 7;
    no-win/no-lose, 7; nonzero-sum, 7;
    obliging, 6, 23–24, 46, 61, 76–77, 94,
    119, 145; positive-sum, 7; problem
    solving, 4, 149; satisfaction of con-
    cerns, received by self and others, 7;
    smoothing, 4; two-dimensional
    model, 5–6; win-lose, 7, 18; win-win,
    7, 18; withdrawing, 4; zero-sum, 7

Tajfel, H., 69
Thomas, H., 107, 141
Thomas, K. W., 4, 5, 50
Thorsrud, E., 70

Thung, M. A., 56
Ting-Toomey, S., 1, 4, 8, 13
Tjosvold, D., 64, 67, 91
Tortop, N., 139
Touzard, H., 19, 28, 29, 31
Trubisky, P., 1, 4, 8, 13
Turkey, 3, 135–151
Turkiye de Orta Dgu Amme Idaresi
    Enstitusu, 139

Uitterhoeve, W., 63
United States, 3, 75, 85, 120
Ury, W., 67, 82, 84, 92
Utley, M. E., 4

Vachette, J. L., 14, 16
Van der Merwe, H. W., 88, 95, 99
Van der Velden, B., 53
Van de Vliert, E., 4, 5, 7, 53, 125, 126
van Epps, P. D., 4
Van Mierlo, H.J.G.A., 55, 56
Van Schendelen, M.C.P.M., 54, 55, 56

Varoglu, K., 149
Verrips, J., 54
Vidal Abascal, V., 108, 110, 112, 113,
    115, 117, 125
Volkema, R. J., 125

Walsh, K., 63
Walton, R. E., 7
Weider-Hatfield, D., 126, 127
Wichmann, R., 33
Wierdsma, A. F. M., 56
Willems, W., 53
Wilson, C. E., 7
Windmuller, J. P., 63

Yang, Z., 1, 4, 8, 13

Zaaiman, A., 88
Zahn, E., 53
Zaleznik, A., 91
Zimmerman, M., 45, 49

ABOUT THE EDITORS
AND CONTRIBUTORS

EDITORS

M. AFZALUR RAHIM is professor of Management at Western Kentucky University in Bowling Green. He is the author of *Managing Conflict in Organizations*, 2nd ed. (Praeger, 1992) and editor of *Theory and Research in Conflict Management* (Praeger, 1990).

ALBERT A. BLUM is professor of Management at New Mexico State University in Las Cruces. He is the editor of *International Handbook of Industrial Relations* (Greenwood, 1981).

CONTRIBUTORS

MANUEL ALCAIDE is professor of economic and management sciences at the University of Seville, Spain.

JONATHAN ALLEN is president of Synexus International, a business consulting firm in Arlington, Washington.

TOMOKO ANDO is a strategic analysis manager in marketing research for Coca-Cola Company Limited, Japan.

BEN EMANS is associate professor of organizational psychology at the University of Groningen, Netherlands.

JUAN GANAZA is lecturer in organizational behavior and human resource management at the University of Seville, Spain.

FRANK M. HORWITZ is professor of business administration at the University of Cape Town, South Africa.

M. KAMIL KOZAN is on the faculty of the department of management at St. John Fisher College, New York.

PETER LASKEWITZ is a doctoral student in organizational psychology at the University of Groningen, Netherlands.

CHRISTOPHER LEEDS is on the faculty of the University of Nancy, France.

ROBERT T. MORAN is director of the Program in Cross-Cultural Communication and professor of international studies at the American Graduate School of Management, Arizona.

LOURDES MUNDUATE is associate professor of social psychology at the University of Seville, Spain.

JOSÉ M. PEIRÓ is professor of social psychology at the University of Valencia, Spain.

JØRN KJELL ROGNES is associate professor of organizational sciences at the Norwegian School of Economics and Business Administration.

MACHIKO SASANO is an assistant trader for J. P. Morgan, Japan.

EVERT VAN DE VLIERT is professor of organizational and applied social psychology at the University of Groningen, Netherlands.

RICHARD WICHMANN is vice-president and executive producer at Videotronics, Inc., in St. Louis, Missouri.